For my wife
and two sons.

Sometimes, the ones who work away never
know how hard it is for the ones left behind.

Book cover design by Ulf Burman – http://mmprod.se/
Cover picture by Security Escort Team 2 with
Eddie Townsley kneeling in the dust
Valhalla by James Brightwell
Editing – Keith Elliott

ISBN 9789151933870
Independently Published
First Edition

STAYING ALIVE

JOHN STEELE

Mosul, January 2005. When life was simple.
There were two choices:
right or wrong.

CONTENTS

Let me tell you something you already know. The world ain't all sunshine and rainbows. It's a very mean and nasty place and I don't care how tough you are, it will beat you to your knees and keep you there permanently if you let it.

You, me, or nobody is gonna hit as hard as life. But it ain't about how hard you hit, it's about how hard you can get hit and keep moving forward, how much you can take and keep moving forward. That's how winning is done!

Sylvester Stallone – *Rocky*

PREFACE

I was in Nigeria looking at a blood-soaked and close-to-death, modern-day pirate who had won second place in a machete fight with one of my soldiers, when I realised it was about time I put my lifetime experiences down on paper.

I did the most stupid things as a kid and somehow survived. I then joined the Royal Navy, qualified and worked as a clearance diver on a bomb and mine disposal team. More than 20 years of commercial diving followed, where both accident and death were commonplace. This was mixed with fast motorbike crashes while racing, then a period of re-education and acceptance as a private military contractor at the height of the troubles in Iraq.

The culmination of this career path led to four years of sea passages off the coast of Somalia, protecting shipping from armed pirates. In 2012, I stepped off a ship in Durban, South Africa for the last time and became a security advisor in the militant-riddled swamp area of Bayelsa State, Nigeria, which brought its own unique challenges.

Finally, my passion turned to trying my hand as a gold prospector in the beautiful, wild countryside of northern Finland, 230km above the Arctic Circle.

Without the crazy people I have had both the pleasure and misfortune to meet throughout my life, nothing in this book would have been possible. There is only one person in this collection of stories whom I will never forgive – I have a very long memory, and karma has an equally long reach.

It all began like this...

Chapter One

THE EARLY YEARS

On a frosty 1961 February morning, I was born in the picturesque Cumbrian market town of Brampton, a few miles east of the border city of Carlisle. I didn't hang around long in the small hospital. Once I was a suitable pink colour and my tubes had been clipped, I was given a clean bill of health and was moved into my grandparents' house with my mum and dad in the nearby village of Hethersgill.

My grandparents were lovely country folk. Grandad Tot could always rustle up a rabbit or a pheasant for the table, and kept big, hairy lurchers for hunting. I only have vague memories of my grandmother. When I was three, she suddenly died and Tot moved into a rented house just outside the village.

I have no idea how legal his hunting was but I learned a lot from visiting him as a small boy: everything from catching trout on a bent pin at the bottom of his overgrown garden to trapping moles in the field behind his house. He used to skin the moles and dry them on the hearth of a roaring fire before selling them to some unknown fur collector.

His lurcher of the moment was called Boy, and he talked to that dog as if it were human. When he headed into the village on his bike, he would just throw a shout of "Watch the house, Boy," over his shoulder as he pedalled away. Boy was all sweetness and light if anyone came to the house while my grandad was away. They would be met with a panting tongue, wagging tail and wriggling body. However, if they tried to leave the house, they would be halted at the front door by a snarling beast that had somehow transformed into the size of a small pony and had teeth that belonged to a werewolf! No-one could leave the house until my grandad came home.

When I was 15 months old and before my grandmother died, we moved from countryside into the city of Carlisle. The house in Grasmere Street cost a grand total of £1200, an awful lot of money at that time. We lived in Carlisle until I was eight. During this period, I joined the Border City Swimming Club and realised how much I enjoyed being in the water. This would reflect on my career later in life.

I could swim 25 yards in 19.3 seconds at eight years old. Even though I was competing against boys two years older and a lot stronger, I had my share of podium finishes. Despite being an eating machine, I was just skin and bone. My mother used to pray that I would get into the water quickly because she was worried that people would think she wasn't feeding me! On my first training session, the coach got us to jump in, climb out, jump in, climb out, repeat, repeat until our arms were burning. Some of the other kids gave up, but I can remember this as the first real test of my personal determination, which I would need later in life to push through many difficult situations.

At weekends, we took the bus to visit Grandad Tot, who had a black rain catchment tank that gathered water from his roof. He occasionally dropped in an eel or two for me to practise my fishing skills. While visiting him one day, I threaded a worm onto my bent pin and dropped it in. I can't remember why, but for some reason, I left the rod and went elsewhere. (I think it was possibly to check the mole traps in the field behind his house.) On my return, I tested it to see if I'd caught an eel. I felt a heavy weight on the end and when the pin broke the surface, there was a shiny silver sea-trout on the end! Overcome with excitement, I unhooked it and ran as fast as I could to the house to show dad and grandad my amazing catch. I remember telling them how hard it had fought and my mammoth struggle to get it out of the tank. It turned out that my dad had caught it in a nearby river the previous evening, and they had hooked it on to my bent pin while I was away! It was stone dead.

At the age of six, I roamed the Carlisle streets with my pal Robert Brown, and was introduced by him and his friends to recreational shoplifting – which I was useless at. We would stuff items up our jumpers then pretend to have a sore stomach and stagger towards a shop door. I can't remember if we ever managed to get away with it, but I know that we were probably Carlisle's worst thieves, and always seemed to have shop staff pounce on us.

Saturday afternoons were always something to look forward to. The ABC cinema had something called the Minors Club. We would rush across town buying penny loaves of bread on the way and watch Flash Gordon, Superman and other amazing flicks. I'm not talking super sci-fi effects, but wobbly black-and-white rockets and jerky puppets. Fantastic stuff to us, though.

The bigger boys, led by Robert Brown's brother, thought it would be a great idea if we blew up an old black car. Somehow, I was nominated for the job. Fuelled by the daring exploits of Flash Gordon, I agreed to carry it out. I was briefed by the big boys, and approached the car in an old car park with trepidation. I was sure my friends had my back but there was a nagging doubt that something was not quite right. Up close, I could see the fuel cap already hanging off, so with a last glance over my shoulder and a thumbs-up at my friends (who were all taking cover), I lit a match and dropped it down the fuel pipe. I was enveloped in a roar of sound and flame. I ran as fast as I could from the scene, crying my eyes out from the shock. My hair was singed and my eyebrows missing. I smelled like the previous Christmas's turkey after my dad had scorched it.

We did the most dangerous and stupid things in our free time. Flattening pennies was a favourite. We would put a penny on the nearby railway track, lie down beside it and watch the train thunder past, just inches away. Another strange notion that I had was the idea that I could fly. I "took off" once from the shed roof of Robert Brown's dad, but my maiden flight was noticeably

4

short and near vertical. This was followed by a blood-dripping bus trip to the hospital for a few stitches on my chin, leaving me with a scar to this day. On another occasion, my mum entered my upstairs bedroom to find an open window with only my fingers on view as I dangled outside. I have no idea what I thought I was doing but I'm sure flight and Superman were involved.

My dad loved the outdoors: fishing, shooting and so on, so he managed to get a job as gamekeeper on an estate near Simonburn, Northumberland. I said goodbye to my friends and we headed over to our new home. My new school in Wark was right next to the River Tyne, and at lunchtime, I took my broom-handle fishing rod under the bridge next to the school, loaded the hook with bread and caught ducks. Forget all of that messing around waiting for a fish: I got a bite every time and a cracking fight from seriously miffed mallards. I know some people are probably shaking their heads now, but this was way before political correctness governed our lives. We would eat live worms and minnows to be "in the gang" and drank out of garden taps and streams. To me, a duck was basically food that went quack.

I was also a bit of a nutcase on my home-made bicycle. Fast was never fast enough. My best friends were Jimmy and George Liddle, the local blacksmith's sons. They lived at the top of a very steep hill beside a stream. A narrow single-track road led to the stream, and an old stone bridge spanned a long drop to the rocks below. One day, we decided that I should see how fast I could pedal down the hill. That's the last thing I remember. The brothers told me later that I got totally out of control on the descent and crashed into the bridge, fracturing my skull. I ended up draped across the bridge wall. A foot or two farther over, and I don't think I would be around today. I woke in Newcastle infirmary after an ambulance dash across Northumberland.

The job was not working out for my dad. Being a gamekeeper to Lancelot Allgood also appeared to include being his slave. So after two years in Northumberland, we headed to south-west Scotland and his new job as a ranger for the Forestry Commission. This mainly involved population control of red and roe deer, rabbits, hares, foxes and all manner of small vermin. It's also where I first learned to pull a trigger.

My new school in the village of Gatehouse-of-Fleet was OK, but being the only English kid in a Scottish school had its challenges. Bits of paper were slipped to me to inform me whom I was going to fight when we finished for the day. Peter Keenan was a name I would often receive, but my most memorable incident was when the bigger boys organised a fight between me and my friend at the time, Donald Cowie, I was sick of my nomination as "duty punchbag" so I hit him from my toes with one right-handed haymaker and laid him out cold. There was a frantic huddle as the older boys tried to wake him up. I got the biggest fright of anyone because I thought he was dead. But we continued to be friends, and I never really got told to fight anyone else after that.

Worthy of mention at this point are the actions of a useless supposed "teacher" called Leon McCaig aka Kipper. To use the term "bully" would be inadequate. He was supposed to be the mathematics teacher at Gatehouse Secondary School. However, he would ignore any kids that could not grasp what he meant with his extremely aggressive in-your-face method of teaching. I lost count of how times he thrashed my hands with his heavy-duty whipping belt over the four years that I was subjected to his constant anger management issues.

My class at Gatehouse. I'm in the second row, 14 years old I think, third from the left.

On one occasion, during a cross-country run, I took a strategic short cut through someone's garden with a friend. We were back early to the school and joined the pack, looking suitably out of breath on our arrival.

Mr Goode, the gym teacher, had been tipped off about our detour by the garden's owner, so we had to be taught a lesson. I was told to go and ask McCaig for his belt so that the gym teacher could thrash my hands. I climbed the stairs to his first-floor classroom and knocked on the door. No answer. I walked in. The classroom was empty. I knew exactly where the belt was, as I had been on the receiving end of it enough times, so I opened his desk drawer and removed it. I walked to the door and put my hand on the handle, but to my horror, the handle moved and McCaig burst in.

"Right, laddie, explain yourself!" he roared. I tried to tell him that the gym teacher had told me to collect the belt but it fell on deaf ears. "Right, laddie, hold out your hand!" he shouted. He delivered three full-strength, up-on-his-toes blows on each

7

hand, then handed me the belt and told me to bring it back when Mr Goode was done. This bully never made me cry as a kid. I just used to stare him out, eye to eye, and absorb it when he beat me. I took the belt down to Mr Goode who gave us one light blow on each hand and sent the other kid who had been caught using the short cut with me to return the belt to McCaig.

It seems strange that when I went on to complete my diving courses in the military only a couple of years later, I walked through the physics and maths parts without McCaig's terrifying (for a child) presence looming over me. It crossed my mind in my 20s to pay him a visit and temporarily stop his clock, but it just wasn't worth it. If you ever read this, McCaig, you horrible creature, I wish you an extremely uncomfortable and painful old age.

On the other hand, there were some wonderful teachers. Mr Sinclair, who is in the above class picture and who almost took a finger or thumb off on the bandsaw in woodwork class, would sometimes dim the lights and tell us wonderful scary stories. Mrs Prentice was the French and German teacher, who at times in the summer had an attractive French assistant whom the pubescent boys used to drool over. But my number one favourite was the mad professor, Jimmy Dent. He'd once had enough of me in a chemistry class and told me to look down a Pyrex pipe arrangement that he'd constructed on a bench. Unknown to me, it was full of flammable gas. He lit the lower end and Whoosh! I got a flashback to when I was six, dropping that match into that car's petrol tank, as a blue flame shot out and nailed my eyebrows yet again!

I was always trying to earn extra money as an early teen. Some of the antics were kept from my parents because even as a kid, I knew they were beyond dangerous. On the first weekend after Easter, some of my friends and I would head to the cliffs and steep drop-offs on the nearby coastline and would climb perilous places to collect seagulls' eggs. These were taken to the nearby fishing town of Kirkcudbright and sold to a fish factory. The eggs were then transported to London in the fish trucks and sold for astronomical prices. How none of us fell off these cliffs,

I have no idea. My youth never included one safety device of any nature, regardless of whatever activity I was involved in.

Another good money-maker, but not at all dangerous for once, was collecting snowdrops in the springtime. These were shipped to London for city dwellers to put on their tables. We would collect 30 or so, put an ivy leaf behind them, flick a rubber band around the bunch and trim the length with scissors. Good, easy money.

Our closest neighbours were Cheetah and Jean, a young couple who cut down trees and lived in a caravan. He got his name from schooldays when he was the fastest runner around. Cheetah owned a Reliant Regal Supervan III three-wheeler, and I joined the couple to go to Dumfries in it to watch live wrestling. I loved those trips, and this progressed to days working with them in the forest during summer holidays. My job was to pull the felled timber from the forest with Paddy, an enormous Clydesdale horse. I was too small to lift his big collar on, but Cheetah would slip it over his head and hook up his chains and leather straps. That horse loved to work. Every morning when we arrived, he would be whinnying and jumping around and I would have to hold him back when I was riding him bareback to the forest on the hill above us.

At the bottom of the hill, there was a stream where he would stop. With me still perched on his back, he'd bend down and suck up gallons of water prior to his day's work. Once up the hill, I would connect the final part of his working chain arrangement, walk him into the forest and hook him up to some timber. If we were pulling spruce, a heavier wood than larch, he would sometimes just rear up, lean forward until the trees were moving, then start trotting through the forest, hauling the timber along. I would run in front holding a rope and lead him through the forest to the closest road, where we would drop the load and make a pile.

He followed me everywhere I ran and would sometimes inadvertently clip my heels with his dinnerplate-sized feet. Every morning, I would have to hold him back, but every evening, his head was down on the way home. Like me, he was completely exhausted but he loved to work.

Towards the end of my time with Paddy, a big shiny blue Fordson Super 6 tractor was brought in with a twin drum winch. The soft carpet of the forest was a difficult place for any tractor, even with four-wheel drive and tyre chains, so Paddy was often hooked up to the tractor, using his body weight to pull it out of the mud. He was an amazing animal.

School was never really enjoyable at any stage of my childhood. When it rained, I would look out of the window and daydream, thinking of the streams rising, where the fish would congregate and what tackle I would need to catch them.

The village didn't appeal as a future place to find employment either. From what I saw, the same people could be found on the same barstools almost every night. I realised that my only future was to escape.

I had noticed the Navy recruitment office in Carlisle, so next time we were in town, I paid a visit with my parents. I was given a few tests that were childishly simple, then told to go home and wait for the result.

Chapter Two

JOINING THE NAVY

GOODBYE HOME

At the tender age of 16, I received an official letter stating that I had passed the tests. I was joining the Navy. I left school for the last time in mid-May after completing my German O-level exam and stopped on the bridge spanning the river Fleet. I ceremoniously opened my school bag in front of my friends and poured its contents of pens and books into the torrent below. This was closely followed by the bag itself. This action made it my happiest day at school since I was five years old. Six weeks later, I began my new life.

I boarded a train in Carlisle with my small suitcase, heading for Plymouth via Birmingham. Somehow between Carlisle and Birmingham, I managed to lose my train ticket, which put me in total flap mode. However, I explained my predicament when the ticket collector appeared and to my relief, he let me off. I arrived with a crowd of other spotty youths in Plymouth, and we were taken over the River Tamar in a bus to *HMS Raleigh*. I was told that I was in Frobisher 27 Division.

For six weeks, we learnt the dubious skills of marching around a parade ground, making our bed to Navy specifications, ironing razor-sharp creases in our clothing and polishing boots to a glass-like finish. After completing this, I was given a preference form with three choices of what I wanted to specialise in. Because of my love of water and swimming, I wrote:

1. **Clearance Diver**
2. **Clearance Diver**
3. **Clearance Diver**

Royal Navy clearance divers carry out a multitude of tasks, primarily involving mine and other ordnance disposal from state-of-the-art mines to WW2 devices. In fact, they are now also deployed far from the sea – in Afghanistan, for example. In my day, their main tasks were mine clearance, general ordnance disposal/attack swims on enemy shipping and underwater maintenance of submarines/ships.

Twelve people from my entry at Raleigh made the same first choice on the preference form. There were only around 200 clearance divers or "CDs" in the Royal Navy at that time, so to my great surprise, I was one of the two chosen to try the aptitude test at Drake Barracks in Plymouth. I was told later that this was influenced by an incident when we were doing swimming tests, where I had held up two guys who were poor swimmers, enabling them to complete the test.

The chosen two turned up at the diving section and we were shown how to clamber into a neck entry Avon drysuit (which was full of holes). A pile of lead was attached to my waist and I was the first to be dropped down a weighted line to the bottom of the pitch-black Tamar. This was my first dive ever, and I remember the sound of dredgers working close by, causing mini flashes of phosphorescence all around my mask. Even though it was blacker than the inside of an ink bottle, I loved being underwater and couldn't get over the sensation of actually being able to breathe down there.

The other guy, who was already shaky after being plummeted to the bottom of the Tamar, freaked out during the decompression chamber dive. He didn't like the sound of incoming air. This effectively removed him from the rest of the day's tests and any hope of a shot at passing the Navy's hardest course.

I passed the aptitude test and was given the opportunity to attempt the full clearance diving course. I was to join the Seaman Diver 19 course (SD19) beginning the following January. But as it was only October, the powers that be decided to send me to Rosyth in Scotland to work on *HMS Abdiel,* the Navy's only minelayer at that time, which was in for a refit.

For a 16-year-old kid en route to join a warship, I was beyond excited. However, the older hands loved to torture new sprogs. On one occasion, my ankles were tied together and I was squeezed into the hawsepipe (the tube that the anchor chain runs down) with a pot of grey paint and a little brush. I did a really good job painting the inside of that pipe until I almost reached the top. The lads had been slowly pulling me up, but with peals of laughter, they let go of the rope and I shot out of the bottom of the pipe like a freshly painted torpedo... Splash! Rosyth dockyard was never the cleanest of water, but there I was in early winter, covered in grey paint, swimming for the nearest ladder with my feet tied together but still holding my paint pot and brush.

I had my first taste on *Abdiel* of what happens to thieves at sea. A bloke had been caught relieving a shipmate's wallet of some cash, and was told to report to the anchor chain locker. This is a foul place in the bottom of the ship's bow, where the stinking anchor chain is stored. The thief turned up and as he climbed into the locker, the hatch was dropped on his fingers. How they weren't severed, I'll never know. He ended up in the sick bay with a pair of mangled hands, but he took the punishment and said nothing. This act of thieving, but more importantly, the consequence, was imprinted in my mind forever. To this day 42 years later, never having met him before or after, I can still remember the name of the mine warfare rating who dropped that hatch.

THE COURSE FROM HELL

After becoming a master paint chipper and ship painter, I headed south on a train for Portsmouth to join the SD19 course, which was run at a 1km lake and wartime torpedo testing facility, Horsea Island.

Initially, it was just a mega stamina test: circuits, diving board, circuits, diving board, circuits, diving board, energy-sapping mud runs with a telegraph pole, then long/short jackstay and endurance swims.

To my horror, I developed an ear infection on week four that put me off-course because I wasn't allowed into the water.

Luckily, I was given the opportunity to join the next course, but I had to start from scratch again as one of 27 applicants.

Horsea Island and the diving board, back in the day

I switched into train-and-prepare mode. It was second time around, so the physical side of the first four weeks was relatively easy. On SD20, fifteen of the original starters remained when we reached week five, called "Live in Week". Other military branches would call it the more apt name of Hell Week. We were allocated 12 hours' sleep time for the whole week, while being constantly mentally demoralised and physically pushed to breaking point. A lot of guys fell by the wayside during Live in Week. You can just make out the crosses in the course photo.

SD20. I am fourth from the right, back row

Course participants are generally crushed mentally and physically from morning to night. You can do nothing right. You are constantly told, "You are shit", and demoralised to breaking point while being freezing cold and way, way, out of your comfort zone. Only the strong of will and character survive it.

Course instructors were always close by to continually let you know that there was no shame in leaving. "A hot cup of tea and a good night's sleep is waiting. Just give the word."

I heard other branches of the military trying to knock the Navy's clearance diving course many times, including the Marines and the Army, especially when I told them that on Live in Week, we started the day off with a 2km jog around the lake. Two kilometres! I would wait for the hilarity to die down, then explain that we were dressed in two woollen undersuits with a diving drysuit over that. A waterproof rubber seal was tightly fitted at your wrists and neck. Over this was the CDBA rebreather diving set. A neoprene hood was placed over your head, restricting any heat loss, and to cap it all, a full-face mask was fitted over your face.

This mask had a small spitcock at chin level that could be turned to either "atmosphere", to breathe air on the surface, or to "gas", which allowed you to breathe underwater. During the 2km run, the spitcock was set to atmosphere, which allowed you to breathe only through a hole a little less than the size of the lower half of your index finger. The mask immediately fogged up, so you had to swish the sweat around to be able to see. However, all the sweat inside the drysuit was contained within and it soon became your personal boil-in-the-bag atmosphere.

Once the run was completed, we quickly entered the water for a 90-minute dive. All that sweat rapidly cooled and began to chill you to the core.

Often the instructors would not allow gloves in the freezing water or even, on occasion, the neoprene hood. Once the dive was over and you came out of the water in a near-hypothermic state, mentally and physically drained, you were told to charge up the diving set manually with what was known as a Haskel pump and get straight back in. It was a tortuous brass and copper contraption: up, down, up, down, up, down on a double seesaw handle; no pushing a button or pulling a start cord.

We would finish a long day of physical endurance, manually pump up our diving sets again and lay everything out in order for the next call to dive. We'd then go for some food. Invariably, a thunderflash would be thrown into the mess hall as soon as we sat down and the petty officers' assistants – or "second dickies", as they were known – would run around screaming "Awkward!" which is clearance divers' code to immediately prepare for the water.

We would stream out of the mess, grabbing what food we could on the way and sprinted to the waterside, totally exhausted, to dress in for the next dive. Our sets would, however, have been drained of gas, while fins, hoods and so on had been totally mixed up and thrown together in a pile. We only had a certain time to enter the water, which was now impossible, so we would then be punished once again with mud runs or some other hideous task. This was constant, and I think you get the picture.

Many quit. For me, I knew that I had to finish the course, no matter what. It was strange, but when someone quit, it would make me stronger. My greatest fear was being taken off it and having the "failed" stigma placed on me. I had nothing to return to, so the only way was forward, no matter what they threw at me. I kept repeating a mantra to myself: "It's only a week", over and over and over.

After those constant mud runs and general physical and mental torture a few weeks of explosives and deep diving training followed. Six of the original 27 starters were left at the end of the course. I was one. At 17 years old I was the youngest clearance diver in the Royal Navy – and proud as punch. Those who have qualified know exactly what I mean. I was told at the time that 96 people originally applied for my course. I have never done anything so difficult in my life since, and on completion, there was no great fanfare for all that toil. We received diving badges to sew onto our uniforms, a diving logbook, a handshake from our course officer George Dance and a quiet "Well done".

But I was accepted. It felt like the doors had opened. The camaraderie and professionalism of the teams flooded in. True teamwork is forged by hardship, pain, blood, sweat and tears. Through that, a friendship is formed with people you have probably never met before but who have been put through the same meat-grinder, and have come out a winner at the other end.

To this day, I am in contact with some of my old team members and former Royal Naval clearance divers who I've never met but are bonded with me because of the course we all completed and the teams that we served on.

PLAYING CONKERS WITH A ROLEX

My first proper draft was to the Clyde Estuary and the Faslane diving team, to work with subsea maintenance on diesel electric and nuclear submarines.

During my time in the Navy, I would be drafted to Faslane twice. The first time wasn't as enjoyable because as a newly qualified "baby diver", you are basically pond life and do all of the menial tasks. One involved a crash between one of our bomb and mine disposal Land Rovers (red wings) and a roe deer. The animal had come off second best and the butchering job was given to me, because the grown-ups thought it would be great fun to see me squirm or worse. But I had shot numerous deer along with many other furry creatures, due to my dad's job as a forest ranger, so I hung the animal in one of the section's showers and gutted and dissected it with my serrated diving knife. One of the petty-officer divers, Scouse Lewis, came in while I was at work and performed an immediate U-turn because as it looked like a very messy murder had just taken place.

One of the most hated punishments was known as a skin swim. If you did anything wrong as a "baby diver", you were ordered to the low pontoons across the road from the diving section. A certain chief diver would order us to strip and swim around in the freezing Clyde waters naked, in full view of everyone passing. This would be conducted until, rubbing his hands together, he had seen enough and let us out. In hindsight, there was definitely something amiss about this, but as a newly qualified kid, he was the chief and I had to comply.

The underwater work was great and pretty much non-stop. We were always on call and I ran up a lot of underwater minutes in my green diving logs. Docking down submarines was fun: lying on my back underwater in the bottom of a floating dry-dock, with a massive nuclear submarine hovering above me, I helped to position the submarines onto large wooden blocks as the huge

19

submerged floating dock was pumped with air and rose in the water, carrying the submarine up and clear of the water. Not many 17-year-olds get to experience that.

On occasion, we had to change the massive seven-bladed propellers on the Polaris nuclear subs, which weighed around 13 tons. We split into eight hours on, eight-off shifts for those jobs. The water was often the best place to be, due to the biting wind-chill on the dockside. I still have a scar on my left hand from the sharp edge of one of those propellers.

One bonus to propeller changes was that at the end of the eight hours, each shift was given an "arduous issue" of one bottle of Pusser's rum, which disappeared very quickly in big white navy mugs.

All CDs were at that time issued a model 5517 Rolex Submariner watch with a NATO strap. Mine was never particularly good at keeping time, despite the name. There was a T on the face that showed that it was made by apprentices, I was told. I have since learned, however, that it stands for tritium, the material used to make the number positions glow in the dark.

I once played conkers with mine in a Helensburgh bar against another CD and ended up with the hands just swinging around uselessly. I handed it into the stores and signed another out, easy as that. Some guys "lost" theirs and drew another from the stores. However, it never crossed my mind to lose mine because of its poor time-keeping.

Recently, I learned that the total estimated number of these models worldwide now stands at around 40, and a recent model sold in America for the princely sum of $178,000. Hindsight is sometimes a wonderful thing. I need to build a time machine.

We regularly left the Faslane base to travel around the west coast of Scotland on deep-diving work-ups. A workup consisted of us diving a little deeper every day until we were hitting our maximum operating depth of 55m, breathing a concoction of mixed gas. The best part of this was drawing our subsistence money (expenses) for hotels and meals that we needed while away from the base. Those meals usually consisted of beer and possibly fish and chips at the end of the night, or a military ration pack, which we always carried on the dive boat. If your luck was in, the hotel would be exchanged for an invitation home from a lucky girl.

As a young diver, I had to pass certain physical tests in a "task book". Once I could perform these satisfactorily to a CD1 (petty officer diver), I would get a signature and stamp and was one step closer to becoming an able seaman, or CD3. The problem was that the CD1s added their own tests into the mix, one being to "steal a girl's underwear and fly it from the mast as we leave port". I managed this one, thanks to many free pints of Stella and some grovelling. I stole a butcher's daughter's knickers after an eventful Saturday night in a Scottish town and flew them from the mast as we left harbour the next morning. The stamp and signature were soon deposited in my task book.

On one workup, our CD1 petty officer Albert Chapman stepped off our 75ft steel diving tender *YoYo* to look for a mine that had reportedly washed up on a Scottish beach. Aggie Dennis, an AB diver, was left to steer *YoYo* around a headland to meet everyone on the other side. I was just ballast at this point in my career, so I was with Aggie mainly for moral support and tea making – or "wet" duties. It went like this:

Albert: "Right, Aggie. I'm going to look at a mine on that beach on Inchmarnock with this farmer. You have the helm and stay away from that rock."

Aggie: "No problem, Albert, *YoYo*'s safe with me."

Me: "Oh, look at that seal up ahead."

Aggie: "Let's run it over!"

Bang!

We had almost ridden clear of the big rock, but now we were stuck fast, with the stern getting higher and higher as the tide dropped. Albert could be seen on the shoreline, a small figure who was extremely agitated, jumping up and down with arms waving in frustration. Once everyone was back aboard, we bore the wrath of Albert and carried all the gas bottles and anything with weight as far forward as possible, until *YoYo* slid forward and dropped off the rock. The prop shaft always ran hot after that.

The old *YoYo* was officially named *RMAS Ironbridge* and is now history. She was sunk as target practice in the Atlantic. Many fond memories went down with her.

RMAS Ironbridge (YoYo)

We had a calm, quiet leading seaman on the team, Kenny Kenyon (RIP). He was the driver of our big diving truck, or "RL". I never knew what "RL" stood for – it just was.

Kenny's problem was his eyesight – or lack of it. When he sat his driving test, he ran over a dog. When he was doing a good deed and pulled over to pick up a hitchhiker, he also ran him over and had to drive him to hospital. The punishment dished out by Albert Chapman to anyone with long hair was a truck ride from the base to a distant Scottish village for a haircut. One of the narrow roads to Arrochar was named the "Wibbly Wobbly Way" for obvious reasons. It had many steep drop-offs to the sea on the left side, and with Kenny at the wheel, it was absolutely terrifying.

One morning, the diving section had a sudden crisis. The only crapper was blocked. No-one owned up, but someone (probably the female Navy Wren writer) had laid what looked like an African babies' arm. It was totally bunged up and the water was up to the top of the bowl. Albert, having been trained in all manner of explosive wizardry, had a solution. We had an improvised explosive device (IED) store with various items that could go bang. He selected the dish of the day, a big cigar-shaped N-Mk5 thunderflash. This was duly wrapped in a spiral of lead to make it sink, the igniter was struck and it was pushed around the bend through the mess with a bog brush. Albert stood back, his brush still dripping, and admired his handiwork with the air of an obvious expert on clearing such blockages.

We all took cover. There was an almighty bang, followed by the tinkling of broken porcelain. He had blown it clean off the wall and into a million small pieces. As the smoke cleared, Albert was still standing in the same position, looking at the gaping hole in the wall where the throne used to be. The only difference was Albert was a different colour. He was covered in a brown mist.

After the section had picked themselves off the floor and stopped laughing, we cleaned up and salvaged the toilet seat. It was washed and "Albert's Triumph" painted on it by a friendly signwriter. The seat was hung on his office wall. It gave us a million laughs and a story – or, as you say in the Navy, a "dit" – to be retold forever.

Albert organised a very memorable trip to Cairnryan, a port on the south-western tip of Scotland. The *Ark Royal* aircraft carrier was being scrapped, and we were there to help remove the propellers. The most memorable incident of that trip for me, though, happened not underwater but in a bar.

The dive team and some civilian divers from the scrapyard were in a local bar, when the shout went up to stage a duck run derby – a Navy bar game. Each team consists of a gunner and a loader. Basically, an empty pint glass is put on the floor at one end of an open space. The "gunner" faces the pint glass, drops his trousers so his arse is exposed and the "loader" places a coin in the crack. The gunner waddles forward and hopefully drops the coin into the glass. Once deposited, he shuffles as quickly as possible back to the loader, who deposits another coin and the whole thing is repeated.

Normally, three coins are used. I was doing well, with two out of two in the glass and the bar cheering me on, when disaster struck. I was about half a length ahead and feeling confident of a win. I got back to my designated loader, Shep Shepherd, for the final run, swung around, bent over and received an instant bolt of pain that made me shoot along the bar, arms flailing. My third coin had been heated with a lighter. Somehow, Shep, without burning himself, had loaded it into my crack. He scarpered, while I got a few ice cubes from behind the bar to cool my blistered money box.

After finishing the *Ark Royal* job and returning to Faslane, I got a shout with another diver called Growth to meet the Boss, a lieutenant-commander diving officer. Almost everyone in the Navy has a nickname, and Growth was named when someone noticed in the shower that he had what appeared to be a third leg. Before meeting the Boss, we both tried to recap what mischief we'd been up to over the preceding few days that might have been discovered. But the Boss simply told us that we'd been nominated to travel to *HMS Gannet* near Ayr and do some helicopter-borne torpedo trials.

We packed our kit, hopped in a section Land Rover and drove there. A flirty and very pretty Wren showed us to our digs and we settled in. It was amazing where those diving badges on the arms of our uniform got us with the Wrens! A few minutes later, we had a knock on the door. The same Wren was standing there with Betty Boop eyes to give us a flight helmet each. She told us to be in the ops room for 09.00 the following morning.

Right on time, we arrived and were ready to go. However, I hadn't realised that there was so much planning involved with any flight: weather, fuel what ifs, etc. etc. The briefing ended and we headed over to the big search-and-rescue Sea King and took off. The route was over the Isle of Arran to an airbase called Machrihanish, where the only US Navy SEAL team on British soil were based. This base was the British version of Area 51 in Nevada. Try to google the goings-on there and you won't get far. The only people who knew what happened there were the people who served on the base.

We were scheduled to land, refuel and push out into the Atlantic to the designated range. A second helicopter would do the torpedo drop, and once the fish was launched, saltwater-activated batteries would run it. The torpedoes had a pre-programmed search pattern. If they found nothing, they would streak away and conduct another search in a different area. Once the power died, they would stop and surface, and would be marked with a coloured smoke float. This is where we came in. Our Sea King would hover over the torpedo while we jumped or were lowered out into the Atlantic. We had what looked like a small hand-held rake that was inserted into a series of holes at the razor-sharp propeller end of the torpedo. The rake was pushed up at 90 degrees, which caused the fins to fold flat. Once this was done and a pneumatic nose cone fitted and locked in position, the torpedo was ready to be recovered. However, when the winch wire was on the way down to lift us, it was vital to allow it to touch the sea before we grabbed it, because thousands of volts of static electricity generated from the chopper had to be discharged somewhere.

Once it was hooked up, we were recovered. On one occasion, Growth was lifted back up on the door winch after the torpedo was secured, then I followed. When I was halfway up, I came to a juddering halt, swinging around in the downdraught above the Atlantic. I looked up and saw the winch-man frantically gesturing for me to lower my helmet's visor. I did, and eventually, I began to be lifted again towards the open door and safety. As I got closer to the chopper, I was covered in a mist of hydraulic fluid. It transpired that the chopper had a hydraulic leak that was also tied into the flight controls, so the pilot was having serious problems.

We flew fast back to *HMS Gannet* and a waiting ambulance, as the winch-man and I needed to have our eyes washed to clear the hydraulic fluid.

The next morning, the weather was too bad for the trials so I was sitting with red eyes taking a cup of coffee next to the ops room. An older pilot and a young pilot fresh from training headed in for their pre-flight brief, and asked if I wanted to join them on their morning flight.

A search-and-rescue Sea King

I had no idea what they were doing, but anything was better than sitting around all day.

I climbed into the back with the aircrew man in charge of the big sonar set and we took off. I watched the coast glide past as we headed south, then we turned inland. I still had no idea what we were doing, so I unplugged my helmet's comms jack, unstrapped myself and walked forward. I leaned my elbows on the top of the pilots' seats to look forward, then realised my comms jack wasn't plugged in. I took it in my right hand, reached up and plugged it in. In that same split-second, my heart almost stopped.

The younger pilot was calmly broadcasting, "Mayday, Mayday, Mayday, twin engine failure." We went into negative G's as the chopper seemed to just fall out of the sky, I dragged myself into a jumpseat, strapped myself in as tightly as possible, my ears continuously bombarded by technical pilotspeak. Suddenly, just as I thought we were about to hit the ground, the pilot flared the chopper and put it down in a perfect landing.

He had been practising auto-rotation, which is what happens in the event of the engines failing. Power is generated in the spinning blades on the way down and then they are flared at the last minute to slow the chopper. You only get one shot at this, which is why constant practice is needed. All three crew members were in hysterics that I had been caught out. The pilot's commentary was only broadcast within the aircraft!

A part of the diving team were called away to participate in an exercise involving *HMS Rothsay* while the ship was visiting its home port, the seaside town of Rothsay on the isle of Bute, off the west coast of Scotland. I was one of those chosen for the exercise, which involved attacking an anchored ship with limpet mines. We were then to be captured, so the ship's company could go through the process of interrogating us and locating our mines.

The original plan was to head out into the bay in darkness and drop two divers out of one of our inflatable boats, or "*geminis*". We would then swim in, using our clearance diver breathing apparatus (CDBA) sets. These were set up on pure oxygen and gave no tell-tale bubbles. We then had to fix mines on the ship's hull, surface at their stern and give up. As we waited for darkness, a storm was gathering over the bay, and by the time we were getting ready to move, there were sheets of rain blowing almost horizontally and large waves. We left the shore and headed out into the storm. As we made our way to the drop-off point, we agreed that there was no point in doing the job underwater. With all the sea spray and rain, the ship's company who were on lookout duties would have a hard enough time spotting two heads with black neoprene hoods in the darkness and stormy water.

We eased into the water ahead of the frigate as our transport backed off and moved away in the darkness. We drifted with the waves towards the frigate's tall bow. As we got closer, we realised that they were tied off on a huge steel Admiralty buoy and were not anchored, as we had first thought. As we drifted closer, a searchlight switched on and was moving over the water ahead of the ship. Maybe they had caught a flash of our inflatable on radar, but as the light swept over us, we put our faces into the sea and the light moved on.

We made it to the buoy that the ship was tied to and decided that to give their divers a hard time, we'd plant our mines on the metal buoy. Once done, we swam to the ship's bow. A guy standing on deck missed us completely. We swam down the side of the ship and once at the stern, we took shelter from the waves. It took the crew about five minutes to spot us. This was followed with a period of not really knowing what to do with us.

Finally, we helped them out by climbing up a stern ladder and allowing them to "capture" us. We were standing on the helicopter flight deck with our hands on our heads, freezing cold, when they decided to remove our dry suits. I explained that there was a special way of removing the suit and I would need one of the ship's divers to help me out of it. Eventually one arrived and as I put my fingers into the wrist seal on my right arm, I pulled out a day-and-night flare and pronounced loudly, "Bang!"

They all fell away from me as I burst out laughing. But in a real situation, it could easily have been a bomb – something for them to process later.

We were then stripped out of our wool undersuits and hosed down with water while standing in our swimming trunks. To the crew, this looked like torture, but the water in that hose was a lot warmer than the sea I had just come out of, and was certainly warmer than the cutting wind blasting over the flight deck. We were then split up. I ended up in a cabin in only my swimming trunks, powerful lights in my face and an unknown number of people behind them.

"OK, son. This how it is. Tell us where your mine is and you can go and head to the senior rates mess on a free bar and drink as much as you like. If you decide not to tell us, I will attach these to your nipples."

Two hands came out of the darkness, past the lights and touched two crocodile clips together in a shower of blue sparks.

My answer was short: "On the admiralty buoy. Which way's the senior rates mess?"

A few hours later, the exercise was complete and the inflatable came to collect us. We were both much worse for wear, and that stern ladder was a lot harder to climb down than it had been to climb up.

Once more, a drain was blocked in the Faslane Base diving section. This time, however, it was not a toilet. An outside drain at the air filling station for the diving equipment was overflowing and needed immediate maintenance as the contents of the drain, along with a horrendous smell, were running down to the passing road within the submarine base. Albert's previous exploits with the toilet blockage were ignored and a plan was hastily put together. If you have explosives on hand and a group of young guys qualified to use them, why go for the boring drain rod use? At least, that was our mindset.

As before, a large weighted N-Mk5 thunderflash was produced and Aggie Dennis and Jock Kerr, the two designated "tradesmen", would be the pair to fix the problem. The team stood at a safe distance while Aggie and Jock carried out both one of the funniest and most stupid exercises I had ever seen. They struck the lead-weighted thunderflash, dropped it down the drain, and then quickly dropped a thick brown coconut fibre footmat over the hole, followed by a sheet of 1/2" plywood. To cap this off, they both stood on the plywood directly over the hole and held on to each other in a sort of man hug.

Five seconds later... BOOM! The blockage was obviously greater than the combined weight of the two knights in shining armour.

The blast blew a hole through the coconut mat and the plywood, and shot up between their bodies, covering each in a film of drain juice. Jock fell over, clutching at his feet and Aggie was standing in a daze, with his eyelids turned inside out. No one could help them, as we were all curled up in hysterics.

Luckily, neither were seriously injured, so we cleaned up and decided to do the sensible thing... we called the maintenance department to clear the drain.

ON BOARD HMS TUPPERWARE

I left Faslane later that year to join the mine-hunter *HMS Wilton* in Portland for a one-year draft. The *Wilton's* nickname was *HMS Tupperware,* due to her construction of glass-reinforced plastic instead of the normal wooden planking. She was the world's first warship to have a hull constructed wholly from glass-reinforced plastic (GRP). The use of GRP gave the vessel a low magnetic signature against the threat of magnetic mines. She was launched in 1972 and was a prototype coastal minesweeper/minehunter for the Navy. Her design was based upon the existing Ton class minesweepers, and she was fitted with equipment recovered from the scrapped *HMS Derriton.*

The year I lived on board was spent mostly travelling around the European coastline with other NATO mine hunters, which was great fun. We once ended up in Loch Awe alongside the jetty, in a small fishing village on the west coast of Scotland. We were having a great time entertaining the (female) population, when our goodwill visit was cut short. We were to take part in a NATO exercise off the Scottish Western Isles.

We reluctantly left the jetty and as soon as we were in calm water, the captain called the engine room to "make smoke". A black chimney of smoke twisted into the sky from our funnel, and in no time, a Canadian jet appeared and "killed" us for exercise. Back to the jetty, pub, and more entertainment! Top man!

The captain once invited some of us into the wardroom for a drink after he'd returned from a run ashore in Bremerhaven. He went down into praying mode on the carpet to demonstrate how to drink a pint upside-down while doing a headstand. He seemed to be taking too much time getting from his knees to the vertical, when a strange noise emanated from his direction. Zzzzzz! Zzzzzz! He'd fallen asleep while kneeling with his head on the carpet!

The gunner on board was Jess Harper. He was in charge of all weaponry and when it came to a replenishment at sea (RAS), his job was to load a blank round into a self-loading rifle (SAR), then fit what we called a donkey's dick – which resembled a yellow dildo with an orange end – over the barrel, and attach a length of thin paracord to the end.

When the Belgian mine-hunter we were working with arrived parallel to us (both travelling at about 10 knots), Jess was supposed to fire the donkey's dick over the other warship and the crew would grab its trailing cord and haul it in. A heavier line, followed by a second, even heavier one was attached and run through blocks on both ships. Material and personnel could then be transferred across the watery gap in between.

HMS Wilton

Jess took careful aim and squeezed the trigger. I watched the yellow projectile arc out against the blue sky to the other warship, a former US but now Belgian-flagged mine-hunter, the *M906 Breydel*. It fell short, glanced off the bridge wing's compass binnacle and flew through an open bridge window, hitting the side of the captain's head. He was knocked out cold and collapsed to the bridge floor. On the *Wilton*, there were a few seconds of silence then an almighty roar as everyone cheered Jess's marksmanship. I turned around to see Jess blowing the smoke off the end of the barrel.

The Belgian captain wreaked his revenge a few weeks later in an unplanned but very dramatic way. The whole hunter fleet was steaming along in the darkness at around 04.00 on a calm sea, in line-abreast formation. The ships were spaced about 100m apart and side by side, moving at around 12 knots. The *Wilton*, being the commanding ship, gave the order for a 90-degree turn to starboard. The inside ships had to slow slightly and the outer ships speed up to allow the line of vessels to carry out the manoeuvre smoothly.

Wilton completed her 90-degree turn to starboard. The vessel on our port side was *Breydel*. She also turned 90 degrees, then

M906 Breydel

100... Suddenly, she loomed out of the darkness, and with a massive impact and an almighty crash of splintering glass-fibre and wood, she connected, heeling us far over to starboard and ripping part of our bow off in the process. I was thrown out of my bunk; alarms were going off. All of our near-constant training came into effect. The fore and aft lower deck messes where we slept were immediately battened down by the chief of the boat, so we headed for the emergency exits.

At that point, the damage control parties were forming quickly and reacting. As I came through the escape hatch, I glanced forward and it was obvious what the problem was. I could see dawn breaking where the bow had once been. The ship's speed was immediately reduced; we broke from formation and wood was dragged forward to shore up the hole in the pointy end. Amazingly, the only injury on the *Wilton* was our radio operator. In a scramble to leave the lower decks, someone ran over him in the darkness and bruised his ribs. There was a perfect flip-flop footprint in the centre of his chest on his white T-shirt! *Wilton* then limped to her home port of Portsmouth, a very sorry sight.

After all the fuss and investigations died down, we headed to Rosyth on the east coast of Scotland to be dry-docked. A new bow was to be fitted, so this was an opportunity for everyone due any leave to take it. We picked a calm-weather window and set off on an uneventful voyage up the east side of the North Sea to our new home for the next couple of months.

We transferred our belongings into *HMS Cochrane,* the shore base attached to Rosyth dockyard. A duty roster allowed a skeleton crew to guard and work on the ship while the dockyard was fixing the bow. One amusing event sticks in my mind. A Scottish mine warfare rating lived around the Perth area and left the ship on Friday afternoon at around 17.00. He drove out of the dockyard on his motorbike, after getting his weekend leave chit signed off. When Monday morning came around, he hadn't shown up for duty. Tuesday morning, still no sign of him. Calls were made but still no joy. At Wednesday lunchtime, he turned up at the gangway on his motorbike. He was told to immediately report to the Jimmy (the officer second in charge of the ship, and as such, the man to hand out any discipline on board). He was asked if he could explain his very late arrival.

"Well, sir, I can explain, but if I told you, you'd never believe me."

"Try me."

"As you know, I live in the middle of Scotland. After my weekend leave, I set off from my mother's house early on Monday morning on my bike, but here in Scotland, there are many hills and glens. I went over and through a few, but as I approached one really deep glen, the air suddenly went very cold and I could see incredibly thick mist ahead. When I drove into the mist, sir, it was Monday morning but true as I am standing here, when I drove out of the other side, it was Wednesday morning."

Everyone fell about laughing. I can't remember the punishment, but it was probably a bit of potato peeling.

Once the new bow was glued on, we conducted a full work-up in the entrance to the River Forth. This entailed testing all systems on board, including the weapons. Jess Harper prepared everything and off we went: Browning 9mm pistols, GPMGs, SLRs and the 40mm (40/60) Bofor were banging away for hours. That night, it was my turn on the stick (mine hunters didn't have a wheel) and the officer of the watch was giving me orders to steer. I could see his mouth working but I couldn't make out a single word. All I heard was Weeeeeeeeeee in both ears! This, along with motorbikes, diving and shooting from inside vehicles in Iraq is probably why I am a double hearing-aid owner these days.

We had a well-known Scottish mine-warfare rating on board nicknamed Eck. I think it was him who, for a laugh, oiled the brake discs on my motorbike, causing me to shoot through Rosyth dockyard gate past the police without stopping. If it had happened today, I would probably have been shot. He was a lovely guy but he liked a dram or two. On one occasion, he came aboard after a serious drinking session and fell down the stairs into the aft mess where he lived. We picked him up and he immediately cracked open a can. The man was unstoppable! By this point, drink-related hunger pangs had kicked in and he was asking everyone for food. For some reason, I had a small cardboard box filled with yellow and white polystyrene packing chips. I pulled an empty crisp packet out of the bin, topped it up with the chips and gave it to Eck. "Aye, yer a guid lad," he said and ate the lot, then fell asleep on the table. Next morning, he was up early and never looked back from his late-night meal of plastic packing chips.

One of our stokers, Tilley Bedford, was leaving to get married. Just before he left, and after all of the good wishes and back-slapping, he was grabbed, held down on deck and given a couple of purple-brown love bites on his neck to explain to the bride-to-be and her family. Nothing was sacred.

Then I left the Navy, though prior to my departure, I was offered a saturation diving course and a car driving course if I would stay (I only had a driving license for a motorbike at this point). In hindsight, I was far too hasty. But I was a young guy who saw a great chance to break into the exciting North Sea diving world. So I opted out and watched as the Rosyth dockyard gates disappeared in the taxi's rear-view mirror. I was chatting to the driver and explained that I had just left the Navy. He gave me the ride to my flat in Dunfermline free!

I am glad to see that the *Wilton* is now safe as a permanent fixture, after being bought in 2001 and fitted out as the new home of the Essex Yacht Club at Leigh-on-Sea on the Thames Estuary. Most of her sister ships have met a sad end at the hands of scrap merchants.

Chapter Three

COMMERCIAL DIVING

21, AND MONEY TO BURN

A commercial diver's life is far from normal. You leave your family and loved ones behind and head to sea, obviously in itself a dangerous place to work. Then you add another level to the danger mix by placing yourself underwater in a totally alien environment, one breath from death.

The public usually think of the job as a warm, clear-water swim, watching passing fish, as per the Discovery Channel. It can be like that – if you are lucky. However, it's more often set in cold, murky or even pitch-black water full of stinging jellyfish or poisonous swimming creatures and on occasion, sharks.

Imagine, for instance, a load suspended on a crane, weighing many tons, lowered to you in the dark, using your surface bubbles as a rough reference. But the tide carries bubbles away from your precise position before they break surface, so it is at best a guesstimate of where you actually are. You are on the seabed, waving your arms around in the dark, until you feel a large suspended mass of metal coming down on you. You have to talk the crane into moving that lump of metal to the unseen job-site and lower it exactly into position. And all the time, you're working in total darkness.

Your air (or mixed gas) hose, communication cable, hot water hose, video cable, lights cable and lifeline are all wound into one single umbilical, and stretch somewhere out in the current, unseen but waiting at any opportunity to be caught on a snag, propeller, or worse, severed by the suspended load as you lower it. It has happened many times.

Diver vigilance goes a long way, but the reaper is quick to pounce. Fingers are all too often removed. Your suspended load is hanging off a crane attached to a ship that is almost never stable; it is usually heaving and pitching, causing the load in your hands to do the same.

If you are a saturation diver, working at the deepest end of the spectrum, you can't just open the trunking and head off to hospital when something goes badly wrong. You must endure decompression that can take days before you are finally able to breathe fresh air and have your injury treated. In Aberdeen and Norway, there are fully kitted operation rooms inside a system that you can be flown to, but this is only a small area of the world's saturation diving. This is why divers are such a close-knit group: they rely on each other as much as soldiers do in battle. All problems are everyone's problems. For me, that is the epitome of team work, not some corporate kayak trip or climbing of a plastic wall to "team build", which at best are just a bit of fun.

I left the Navy on my 21st birthday to pursue a career in commercial diving because the money was a lot better. To give some idea, I was now earning £512 a week, whereas the Navy had been paying me £336 a month a couple of months earlier. My first job was with Northern Divers in Glasgow and the work-site was Yarrow shipyard, blowing a concrete sill off a drydock that was being refurbished.

I arrived at Glasgow Queen Street railway station in March 1982 from Dunfermline, where I bought a small flat and set up home with my girlfriend Linsay Russel. Bernie Mumby and Pete Waller, two of the divers, told me that as the Apsley Hotel where we were lodging on Sauchiehall Street was full, we had to eat breakfast at a neighbouring hotel. So next morning, there I was, excited about my first working day out of the Navy, sitting in the next-door hotel and tucking into a full greasy breakfast with a mug of tea. I was wondering where the other guys were when out of the corner of my eye, I noticed Bernie, Pete and the other clowns peering through the dining-room window from the garden. They had finished their breakfast in the Apsley and were waiting to see what would happen to me when the hotel rumbled that I wasn't a paying guest. I came clean to the waitress, paid for my breakfast and started my first day out of pocket – but a bit wiser to the antics of the lads.

A bar strategically placed just outside the dockyard gates was called rather unimaginatively The Dry Dock. Every lunchtime, pints were pre-filled and stacked one on top of the other for the one-hour drinking frenzy of swearing Glaswegian dockyard workers. There were also a lot of items that had been "found" for sale in tucked-away plastic bags – everything from roast beef to rig boots were available for the right price; it was a den of friendly thieves.

Scrap metal was continuously leaving that dockyard. In fact, "scrap" was not the word I would use. Some of the pipework was marked "hot" because it had just been freshly fabricated and was meant to have been installed on a frigate that was being built, not taken off to a dodgy scrappy to be melted down. No wonder ship-building has declined in the area.

We finished early in the dock one day and decided to participate in the hotel's afternoon high tea. The dining room filled with a section of elderly Glaswegians who seemed quite well off. All was going well until, after sipping on his Earl Grey tea and nibbling on a cream cake, Bernie Mumby leaned to the side and let rip a fart that could be heard two blocks away. There was instant silence but my table all fell about laughing. Bernie never even blinked and as one shrivelled creature scowled at him with beady eyes, he held his thumb up to her.

The staff were summoned and high tea was over for us. We were banned from all future afternoon events with the blue rinse brigade. We were grudgingly allowed breakfast and dinner, but only on condition that there was no more trumpeting action.

A STAR WARS SUMMER

After Glasgow, I got married in the Dunfermline Town Hall and had a quick honeymoon in Blackpool. I was called shortly after and given the opportunity to work for a company called Global Diving. I headed to Aberdeen and the operations manager informed me that if I was willing, he had a contract through the summer season aboard the brand-new yellow diving support vessel *Seaway Condor*. The next day, I boarded a chopper bound for the Heather Alpha where the *Condor* was working.

We touched down on the platform and the helicopter liaison officer directed us off the helideck. Two of us were destined for the diving support vessel, so a cargo basket was rustled up and with our bags and spares, we were swung out from the platform to be dropped onto the ship's deck. Suddenly, we came to a juddering halt, swinging out over the sea. This would normally have been OK – however, we had stopped right in front of a roaring red-hot flare stack. We were effectively being barbecued. A flurry of people with toolboxes were running around the crane, trying to sort the problem out. Eventually, we got moving again, and we touched down on the *Seaway Condor's* deck, minus a few pounds of sweat.

For me, this was like Star Wars. The diving support vessel (DSV) had port and starboard saturation diving bells and an under-deck moon-pool for air diving. I was allowed a free phone call per week from my bunk, the food was fantastic and I loved it. I was 21 years old and living the dream.

I learned a valuable lesson on this job that could have ended very badly. I was working at the 50ft level, wire-brushing a node prior to it being photographed, but the tide was running hard, which put a lot of drag on my umbilical. I pulled around 15ft of slack in and, following a tip I had overheard from one of the old sweats, I had brought a few welding rods in my knife sheath. I fastened my 15ft of slack off with a twisted welding rod around the umbilical and an anode leg. This gave me almost five meters of freedom to move freely around.

Unknown to me, engineers on the DSV were having teething problems with a dynamic positioning system, which allows a vessel to stay in one position using only thrusters and satellites. If there is a malfunction, however, the default setting is to move away from the platform. This is exactly what happened – at speed. One minute, I was using the hydraulic wire brush, and the next, my welding rod straightened and pinged off my umbilical. I was dragged through the water, bouncing off every horizontal member on the platform. Luckily, I made it out without hanging up on anything but the hydraulic brush wasn't so lucky. It caught on something and was torn off the end of the two hydraulic hoses connected to it. Lesson learned: always have a clear exit.

After writing this, a friend told me of a dramatic diving documentary film called *Last Breath* that had just been released. I watched it and can relate to the film exactly, as what happened on board the *Bibby Topaz* happened to me on the *Seaway Condor,* but luckily for me, without the unwanted drama. The only thing that died in my episode was the hydraulic brush.

Global merged with Svitzer, a salvage company from Denmark, and became Svitzer Global. I got my first taste of pipe-laying with them aboard an old laybarge, *Castoro 5,* in the Storebælt off Denmark. The controlling company was Danish Oil and Natural Gas, or as it was displayed on the back of their workers' coveralls, much to our amusement: DONG. We laid a pipeline through dunes onshore and headed to sea, leaving a trail of concrete-covered steel pipe behind us. Pipe-laying, from a diving perspective, is easy money. It just meant a couple of dives per 12-hour shift to check the angle of the "stinger" on the stern. The stinger looks like a tail at the stern of the barge, it is a series of rollers on a hinge that can be raised or lowered to change the pipe's curve to the seabed as it's laid out behind the barge.

This barge was run by Italians. There were waiters and even wine waiters. Every meal had a bottle of red wine and a bottle of white at the table. We would get the lads who didn't drink to sit away from us on a different table, and we would re-cork our bottles, hide them, join the non-drinkers and sneakily re-cork theirs! The bottles would then be stashed until we were off shift, where they were enjoyed in one of the cabins!

I was on board the *Castoro V* when the Germany v Italy World Cup Final took place. The Italians stopped pipe-laying, capped the end of the pipe and laid it on the seabed, effectively halting all work so both shifts could watch the game. The Italians won, so an impromptu party took place and everyone appeared the next day looking worse for wear.

Once the pipe-laying was completed, I was relaxing at home in Dunfermline with Dave Donaldson, a fellow diver. My flat was very small and the kitchen/living room was open-plan. I was talking to Dave as I washed a couple of glasses about to be filled with vodka, when there was a knock on the door. "I'll get it," he said. I heard a man and woman's voice and Dave invited them in. As soon as I saw them, I realised: Jehovah's Witnesses.

They started to tell us about when and where they held their prayer meetings and asked if would we like some brochures, but Dave stopped their flow by asking, "Do either of you have a Bible with you?" They nodded and the man pulled one out of his small bag.

"Ok," said Dave, "I would like you to open it at *Mark 16:18*." They complied and he asked the man to read it out. It went something like this. "They will pick up snakes with their hands; and when they drink deadly poison, it will not hurt them at all; they will place their hands on sick people, and they will get well."

Dave walked into my kitchen and pulled a blue bottle of bleach from under the sink. He poured it into one of the glasses I had been washing, placed it on the coffee table and said, "Drink that, and we will be in your church on Sunday."

They packed up and left. Not one more word was spoken.

I have since heard that the Jehovah's Witnesses have modified their version of the Bible to take this out, as it was an old favourite of non-believers. But how can they just modify a book that is a record of events from thousands of years ago? How many times have people just decided to change it over all that time to accommodate their own beliefs or feelings?

The chance of a job in the sun came up after the pipe-laying, so I grabbed it with both hands. DULAM Diving in Dubai was looking for divers, and with winter approaching, I packed my kit and joined an old dive boat with a charismatic crew sailing from Sharjah.

As a keen young diver, I was paired up with an old hand, Taff Williams, for my first dive. We prepared our scuba equipment, hopped into the Zodiac inflatable boat and headed to a marker buoy tied to the pipeline where the last pair of divers had finished their inspection swim and had tied it off. Visibility was very good and there were no strong tides to hinder our progress. Both of us simultaneously went over the sides into a fish-filled, silent blue world. I followed the buoy line down to the pipeline and looked up. I was at 30ft and could see the inflatable above. Taff was alongside me. As the new boy on the team, I would be doing the donkey work and pulling the buoy along. I undid the buoy's knot, tied a quick bowline loop, slipped it onto my arm and checked my compass.

Once I had confirmed which direction we were heading along the oil pipe, I gave a thumbs-up to Taff and set off at a strong pace. I wanted to give a good impression to the dive team and push out a good distance along the pipeline.

We were looking for any abnormalities in the pipeline. The pipeline was constructed from lengths of concrete-coated steel pipe to keep it heavy on the seabed and as such, needed to be inspected regularly. As I passed every welded section, or "field joint", I marked it off as OK on my scratch board. I was so engrossed in the task that I just presumed Taff was swimming alongside me – so imagine my horror when I turned and there was no Taff!

My head was searching everywhere. Shit! First dive in the Gulf and my buddy had been eaten by a shark! I had no idea where he had gone, so I headed back along the pipe. About five pipe lengths back, I began to make out a figure. There was Taff, fins off, arms outstretched and walking slowly, one foot in front of the other along the top of the pipe.

So we continued at Taff's pace, inspecting each field joint. When our air was getting low, we tied the buoy off around the pipeline and surfaced to another glorious day in the Gulf. Taff's first words to me in his thick Welsh accent when he spat his demand valve out were: "No rush, boyo, no rush."

MAN OVERBOARD

Taff, a stocky, shaven-headed, broken-nosed drinking machine, was one of the Gulf diving legends. He would do you no harm – unless you crossed him. His big story (that could surely be made into a movie) was when he fell off a vessel at night, and it sailed on over the horizon, leaving him alone in a flat calm sea in shredded underpants. When I started writing this book, I wanted to include people around me who had done something out of the ordinary, and it is hard to top this one. In Taff's own words, it went like this:

"We had berthed at the IMS jetty (Dubai) early in the morning to load on victuals, grab some shopping and get the air-conditioning fixed. We had been offshore for about six weeks, so we were raring for a beer. We completed our work in the morning, so at 12:00, we left the vessel for some shopping and grog. We were sailing offshore at 20.00, so as usual, we tried to drink as much as possible in the short time allowed. Mission accomplished, we climbed back on board the supply vessel about 19:30 and at 20:00 cast off and proceeded to the Umm Shaif field.

"I had something to eat, then weaved my way to bed, feeling quite happy with myself. A warm belly full of beer and vodka: what more could you ask for? A couple hours later, I woke up. The AC had still not been fixed and I was sweating heavily. All the grog was leaking out of me and I felt like I was melting! I decided to sleep on the deck, but in hindsight, this turned out to be a very bad idea in marginal weather and a pitch-dark night.

"How it happened I don't remember, but I recall that I had gone onto the bow to sleep in the breeze. Being an old vessel, it didn't have a steel bulkhead, but railings along the bow and side. I think I was sleeping on the deck. However, I turned over in my sleep at some point, slid under the bottom rail and took a fall into the water.

"I remember rolling down the ship's side with the force of the water keeping me in place. I was being torn to shreds by barnacles and other marine life growing on the side of the vessel. I only had a pair of shorts on. Everything was happening so fast, but I managed to get my feet onto the hull and pushed myself off and down. I was terrified the propellers were going to get me but eventually I surfaced. The ship was about 100 metres ahead of me.

"I started screaming and shouting like a banshee but to no avail. There was no one on the dark deck to hear me. The first thing that went through my mind was: 'You've really fucked up here, boyo. What the hell are you going to do about it?'

"The only practical thing to do in a situation like this is to keep your head together, stay afloat and stay alive. I remember thinking: 'fuck it's dark: no moon, not even any starlight.'

"Morning came, and soon the sun was beaming down on my bald shaved head. I was gagging for some water. A thought crossed my mind about water, water everywhere but not a drop to drink. This was exactly my predicament. I had already decided that I wouldn't swim – no point to it. I had no idea how far, or even in which direction the beach or nearest offshore structure was.

I floated as best I could while keeping my head above water. The sea by this time was a bit choppy and the hot wind was like a mild hairdryer.

Around what I assume to be midday as the sun was directly above me, I could feel my head burning and already blistering. My mouth and eyes were being damaged by the salt water so I needed another plan – and fast. As a diver, it became obvious that due to my rapidly worsening condition, the best place would be underwater. The seas were calming down, so it was easier for me to float. By filling my lungs and just letting go, I found my natural buoyancy was just below the surface, so I took a breath, let go and floated with my head just under the surface. When it was time to replace the air in my lungs, I just gave a gentle kick, surfaced, took a breath and sank again. Not only did this protect my head from the sun but was also of benefit because my eyesight was going. My eyelids were swollen shut and I couldn't see a thing.

"As sound travels farther in water, I figured it was the best place to hear a rescue vessel coming. I heard a couple of vessels in the distance, but no one came for me. Many things go through your head when you're treading water in the middle of nowhere. During the roll down the ship when I fell in, my shorts had been ripped to bits, so my tackle was exposed, I had my nuts in my hand the whole duration of my ordeal, and small fish were feasting on my shredded arms, legs and torso, I didn't want them to also have my nuts on their menu!

"By now it was getting dark again, and it looked like I was going to have another night in the Gulf. I spent it treading water, listening intently for any sound of an engine and feeling slight tugs all over my body, where small fish were still picking and feeding on my torn flesh. Thoughts of sharks crossed my mind, but were dismissed immediately: no negative thoughts allowed. I made all kinds of promises of life changes that I would take when I got out of this massive fucking bath.

"Morning came and the seas were down. I remember a big seagull or something dive-bombed me. It must have thought I was breakfast. Then I heard it: a vessel's engine in the distance. My heart leapt. I was feeling a bit tired by this time. I'd been in the water for two nights and it was beginning to take its toll on me. I let myself sink again and I could hear underwater that the vessel's engines were getting louder and nearer, so I popped my head above water and started waving my arms and shouting as much as I could, considering my lips and tongue were swollen like balloons.

"I went under again and heard the vessel was much closer. The engines were revving down. A couple of minutes later, I heard another noise, a higher-pitched engine. They had launched a Zodiac. I was going to be all right. I could hear them shouting that they had seen me and finally, I felt hands grab me.

"By this time, I must have been a real sight. My eyes were swollen shut, my lips were badly cracked and bleeding and my tongue was swollen and painful. I had barnacle cuts all over my body that had been cleaned up by the fish and I was practically naked. I didn't want these Indian sailors thinking that the Welsh were a small-dicked race, so I refused to let them pull me into the Zodiac until they gave me a pair of shorts, or something to hide my private parts. They eventually dragged me into the Zodiac and took me back to their supply boat.

"When I arrived on the boat, I drank as much water as I could without vomiting. They took me to a big offshore platform called Zakum Central, where I was then medevaced via chopper back to Dubai. I was off work for about a week, and then went back offshore to work.

"I received my salary couple of weeks later and due to my unplanned absence, the office staff had docked me two days' pay!"

This was only one of Taff's stories. Another was when he left home to head out to the Gulf from Wales, had a stopover in Paris and never arrived in Dubai. He was later seen on TV demonstrating with students in Paris: placard, the lot, and three sheets to the wind!

OUR "DIVE AID" SCAM

I returned to work with Svitzer Global, caught a flight to Esbjerg to join the dive support vessel *British Enterprise 5*, an ex-oilfield supply vessel that had been converted to accommodate diving/mini-subs. She had a large hangar on the back that made her top-heavy and caused her to roll alarmingly, even on a flat sea.

Our main task was to act as underwater garbage men. We travelled around the platforms in the Nam and Dan fields and recovered metal scrap off the seabed. This was to combat the effects of corrosion and electrolysis on a platform, the technical details of which I won't bore you with. On one of these dives, I encountered a large specimen of the *Anarhichas lupus* family, a big grey fish commonly known as a wolffish, which is famous for its fearsome dentistry. This outsized specimen had taken up residence under an extended overspill beside one of the platform legs. It was easy to spot its residence, because the entrance to its dark cavern was littered with shell fragments that it had chewed up with its powerful jaws and large teeth that protruded from its mouth at odd angles. Every time I went close, it would glide out to protect its territory. But wolffish are very good to eat. We were living off slop served up by an alcoholic Scottish cook at that point, so I asked the surface to construct a spear, to turn that aggressive fish into lunch.

A spear was thrown together and lowered 140ft down to me. The lads were gathered around the dive supervisor's monitor, transmitted from the camera on top of my Kirby Morgan 17 helmet. I waddled towards the dark cavern and on cue, this toothy eel-like shape slid out to threaten me, and I thrust my harpoon at it as hard as I could. The spear went straight through the fish's head and I thought that was that. Wrong! My problems had just started. The nightmare creature was smashing its big mouth open and closed and was swimming towards me, impaling itself further on the spear that I had stupidly tied to my wrist. Just as I could feel the wash from its snapping mouth in a swirl of my bubbles and squeals, I managed to free the spear and it swam off. The show was over but the lads were all in stitches. They reminded me of that incident at every opportunity.

That alcoholic cook was a nightmare. I came into the mess one morning for breakfast, prior to starting my shift, and ordered some eggs and bacon. He just sat there looking vacantly at the tea urn. Weirdo, I thought, as I dropped a teabag in my mug. I then went over to the urn to pour in some hot water, grabbed the handle to release the water and received the biggest electric shock I think I have ever experienced. The cook rolled around in peals of laughter. "I did that; I did that," he slurred through his alcoholic stupor. Instead of warning people or even better, turning it off, it provided his morning entertainment.

After I had moved from that job, I heard that he died on board. The lads laid him out in the galley's vegetable chiller room, sailed across the North Sea and dropped him off stiff in Edinburgh's Leith docks. I secretly hoped it was the urn that got him.

Working for a few civil engineering diving companies, I travelled around small harbour towns of Scotland doing subsea construction work. On one occasion, I pulled a job on the Isle of Skye in the village of Kylachin. The job was easy enough and a load of laughs. We were employed to fill underwater gabions. You have probably seen these on the sides of highways. They are basically rectangular steel mesh cages containing rocks. The ferry slipway was being eroded by constant waves and wash from the propellers, so the gabions were to be built along the ramp sides in an attempt to stop this happening.

At this time, Live Aid was in full swing and everyone (not me) was full of "Feed the World". So we devised a cunning plan to supply a fund for our beer and bar lunch every day. We were using a home-made freeflow diving helmet, a sort of glass-fibre version of the old copper diving helmets. Every time a ferry was heading to the slipway, we would tell the diver to come out of the water and we would then lower the diving flag at the top of the ramp to show the ferry that a diver was clear. The diver would then sit on a chair on the ramp and theatrically drape a piece of seaweed over his helmet. We placed a bucket beside the chair with some loose change inside, and he would pick up a placard reading: "Forget Live Aid: remember Dive Aid. Act now! Every penny counts!" We always had a diver ready to jump on the ferry, do a quick U-turn and lead passengers off. As he passed the seated diver, he would stop and drop a few coins into the bucket. This prompted a chain reaction: people were even taking pictures with the diver and slowly filling our beer bucket up with loose change. We never forced anyone to do it; it was all for a good cause. Ours.

This gravy train came to an end when the ferry's chief engineer, a very religious man, told us that if we didn't stop, he would call the police. The resident engineer, a clown at the best of times, agreed with the chief. That night, or should I say early morning, we took the left-over sandwich scraps from the bar and as we passed his caravan, we lobbed the bread onto his roof.

As dawn cracked, every seagull in Kylachin was battering out a drum solo with their webbed feet on his caravan roof. Alfred Hitchcock's *The Birds* had nothing on this. Next morning, he complained bitterly about the birdlife singling out his caravan. We carried it on for about a week before he caught us, but by then, his caravan was fully glazed in a yellow feather-coated streaky mess and stank of rotten fish.

THE PERILS OF ELEPHANT BEER

In 1984, I got divorced after having married when I left the Navy at the grand old age of 21. We had moved back to Gatehouse of Fleet in southern Scotland because property prices there were too good to resist, and I bought a beautiful 17th century cottage, Barhill Lodge. My wife's maiden name was Linsay Russel, but it should have been Jackie Russell. While I was away earning money for our future, my wife decided that a bloke dressed in rags who shovelled cow shit on a local dairy farm was a better bet. But I wasn't bitter. Much.

The day before I discovered her extra-marital activity, I had bought a Browning 5 shot semi-automatic shotgun (it was legal at that time) with the same dairy worker from a local gun shop. He must have been a worried man! I found out what had been going on at about 2am the following day, and phoned him to come round. Believe it or not, he did.

I was waiting at my kitchen door when he pulled up on the far side of the parking area. He flicked out the bike's side-stand and walked towards me, taking off his helmet as he approached. He then stopped, looked at me, then back at the bike, and said, "The f***ing choke's sticking on that thing." To this day, I have no idea why I didn't batter him all over the parking area (or worse). But I didn't. I have never set eyes on her since.

While waiting for my divorce to be finalised, I arranged to go to the pub with my father. I walked through the forest to his house, but the beer was calling and he had already set off to the village. I wanted to catch him up, so I stole my brother's unrestricted 50cc Suzuki AP50 moped and set off in a cloud of two-stroke smoke, down the network of forestry roads to the village. Once I reached the outskirts, I embedded it in one of the many rhododendron bushes in the area and walked into the bar. The owner told us that she had a canned beer that wasn't selling, so if we wanted it, it was on the house. It was called Elephant Beer; it was Danish and 8.5%.

A few hours and many free cans later, we staggered from the bar. As we weaved to the end of the village, my father was going to continue on the long route via the main road to his house. "No need," I slurred. "I've got transport." He followed me to the rhododendron bush and his face dropped as I pulled out the taxi home. I kick-started the bike, pointed it in the right direction and told him to jump on. There were no rear foot pegs. Imagine the picture: me on the front, half sitting on the fuel tank and my dad in a three-piece suit, his knees bent and his hands inside the back of his trouser bottoms, holding his feet off the ground.

We got moving and were tearing past the trees and bouncing over potholes on the forestry roads, laughing our heads off, until we arrived at the entrance to a battery chicken farm. The trucks servicing the farm had been taking a wide turn to enter and had left deep tyre tracks at the side of the road. One minute, all was well with the world, the wind in my face and 50cc of snarling fury between my legs; the next, I took a sharp unplanned swerve as the front wheel followed a wayward tyre track.

As I made contact with the ground, the breath was knocked out of my lungs and I hit something very hard with my right side. I was waiting for my breath to return, gasping like a fish out of water and I heard my father gasp, "John, are you all right?" I can't remember my reply, but I remember staggering to my feet, picking the moped up and kicking it back into life. As the headlight flickered on and shone its pitiful light on the road, I was met with the sight of my father facing me on all fours, the knees and elbows torn out of his suit and blood dripping from the chin of a gravel-encrusted, blood-smeared face, because that was the first part of him that had contacted the road.

The beer told us to get back on board, so we continued the journey back to his house and I carefully placed the scuffed moped back where I'd found it. I borrowed a torch for the last part of my hike home, but halfway, I had to stop for a pee. I happily relieved myself, writing "Elephant Beer" in the air with the flow, but when I zipped up my jeans and bent down for the torch, I noticed the ground was covered in blood: my blood. I was peeing it. I sobered up immediately and quickly walked the rest of the way. Once in my house, I convinced myself that a cup of tea would fix it. Not so. My next visit to the toilet turned the bowl red, so I did what seemed the obvious thing to an injured, drunk man: I went to bed.

Next morning, there was no change, so I took my clanging hangover to a doctor and was diagnosed with a bruised right kidney. I drank a few gallons of water and it eventually cleared up. I have never drunk Elephant Beer since, although I sometimes see it tucked away for sale and wonder if I should try it, just for old times' sake.

Left in the empty house kicking my heels, I realised things would need to be split two ways, so I made it easy – with a chainsaw. I left behind a pile of ash from my half of the contents in the parking area. The walls were 1m thick and made of stone so even if I wanted to, I couldn't split the actual house with the tools available. I tried my best to sell the house at a loss, as I had just been offered a one-year contract in Saudi and finding diving work at that time was no problem. However, someone decided to pay over the asking price and I had to grudgingly give my errant wife £1200, which was half of the profit.

I took a one-year Saudi contract and flew east, easily forgetting these problems. I was a free spirit again. The job was three months on, one month off, and was just what I needed: loads of laughs with the lads, a decent salary and paid on time, for once. We sailed up and down the Persian Gulf side of Saudi, servicing and constructing subsea equipment from pipeline swims to setting jackets, which resemble small oil rigs, and all manner of jobs in between. I fished a lot in the evenings when the ship was at anchor after a day's diving, and caught fish that sportsmen pay a fortune to pursue, from big sharks to sailfish, tons of barracuda and various members of the jack family. A lot ended up on the ship's barbecue, much to the joy of the crew.

NEARLY KILLED BY FISH GUTS

When my year in the sun was up, I returned to the UK and ended up working for Northern Divers in Broughty Ferry, near Dundee, where we installed a new sewage outfall pipe in the middle of the river Tay. I hooked up with one of the guys I had worked with in Saudi: Sean Marshall, a tall, skinny bloke from Braemar. He had a bike, I had a bike, and we got on like a house on fire. I followed him to Aberdeen and we had a ball, drinking, partying and generally living life to the full. He knew a nurse and she had a pal. Before long, I had bought a flat that was strategically situated above the Hawthorn bar. The nurse's pal – Tracy Georgeson – moved in.

Just before Christmas 1987, I was on an underwater welding job in Invergordon, near Inverness. This town was rife with lively characters, thievery and a recurring theme of endemic idiocy, fuelled through a general alcoholic haze. To give you some idea, the town's Christmas lights were stretched down the high street between light poles smeared with axle grease to stop locals stealing them.

We convinced a local café owner known as Smelly Willie to give us as many of the days leftover cakes and so on that would otherwise have been thrown away for £2 each, and eat as much as you like. We told him that we were the advance party to a huge group of workers coming in a few months, which was bending the truth by a huge margin. I never knew if he actually believed us, but he was still making some profit from his scraps.

Our regular drinking haunt was a working man's bar on the main street owned by a big, friendly Irishman. One freezing day, we were having lunch and a few beers in his bar after a morning working in the ice-cold waters of the Beauly Firth. One thing led to another, and we convinced the dive supervisor to continue the working day by staying in the pub. He was never a big drinker and was easily led astray after a few sherbets. The afternoon became evening and the supervisor was properly pissed. My mate GK was wearing my woolly bear – the Navy name given to a thick one-piece woollen undersuit that divers wear under a drysuit to keep them warm. So picture the scene: he was wearing white long-john thermal underwear and my bright red woolly bear, sleeves tied around his waist, and was playing pool. Suddenly, the pub doors burst open, and in filed a load of women – the bar's female darts team. They practised for about 30 minutes, then the opposition team turned up.

As we were new boys in town and living it up, most of the combined darts teams' attention was focused on us. We were loving it. The barmaid had a flat upstairs and a party was organised for when the bar closed. By 9pm, the dive supervisor couldn't even walk. One of the opposition darts team shouted out, "Dinnae let this yin escape; ah'll be back in a jiffy." There was no chance he was going anywhere under his own steam anyway. Fifteen minutes later, she turned up with his taxi –a stolen Asda supermarket trolley. He was last seen being pushed through the frozen streets of Invergordon by a woman with rubbish tattoos and a flabby beer belly!

Last orders were called in the bar and as planned, we all bought beer carry-outs and headed upstairs to a flat filled with Christmas decorations. The music was loud and the beer flowing, but by around 2am, everything was coming to an end. I ended up kipping on the sofa. GK had disappeared, location unknown. I woke around 8am with a banging headache and bailed out. We had to catch up with the work we had skipped the afternoon before. I made my way to the dock and the supervisor was already there. But GK was "missing in action" and as he still had my woolly bear, I couldn't dive.

Around 10.30am, we saw a tall figure in a red woolly undersuit carrying two plastic bags. One was loaded with bread rolls; the other, orange juice and milk. His first words were: "You're never going to believe this." We crowded round to listen. Apparently, towards the end of the party, he had sneaked off to the bedroom of the girl who owned the flat and spent an eventful night there. But when he woke, he decided to make a stealthy exit.

He swung his legs out of the bed, quietly slipped into his white long johns and white long-sleeved thermal top. Next was the bright red woolly bear. He quietly pulled himself into it but suddenly developed a sense being watched. He turned his head, and at some point in the night, the girl's small son had climbed into the bed beside her. Their eyes met and the boy whispered one word. "Santa!"

After the Invergordon job, diving work was scarce because it was winter. A friend's brother, who owned a legitimate loans business in Aberdeen, asked if I could help with a little repossession work. Most were sub-contracted from a large and well-known bank and were resolved quickly, because the bank usually had a spare key for the vehicle. But one incident definitely did not go our way. We were tasked with repossessing a car belonging to a family of well-known scrap merchants in a rundown area. We first informed the local police because of the notoriety of the family involved. We wanted them to be on scene as we removed the car. They point-blank refused. This should have been the first combat indicator. However, we pressed on. A recovery truck was put on standby and was supposed to be circling the area, ready to arrive on scene when we gave them the green light.

We pulled outside of the defaulter's house and my friend's brother, dressed in a suit and tie, knocked on the door. There had already been a lot of furtive curtain movement as we approached the house. The door opened and a woman appeared. By-passing dialogue, she switched straight to abuse. A writ was thrust at her and she took it. That's it: game on. As soon as anyone physically accepted the writ, we could go ahead with the repo. My friend and I unloaded the vehicle of all possessions and made a pile on the pavement while my friend's brother frantically called the recovery van – but to no avail.

The female owner of the car had come out of the house and was swearing and shrieking, which could be heard all over the neighbourhood. Half the street were turning out and becoming angrier by the minute. We waited for the recovery truck for as long as we could, but men were arriving by now, and it got to the point where there was going to be a lynching. We were forced to retreat to our car and escape.

Repo work didn't bother me from a moral standpoint, because the vast majority of the people taking loans from the friend's brother's shop did it as a way of life, with no intention of paying it back. In fact, some would take a cash loan, leave the office and head straight over to the betting shop on the opposite side of the road for a flutter on the horses.

Then out of the blue, I got a phone call. I was needed to fill a diving position in the Scottish Orkneys on a remote island called Flotta. The big oil company Occidental had a refinery there with a big single-buoy mooring system for connecting tankers and filling them with processed crude oil. The large steel pipeline that ran from the refinery down to the shoreline and out over the seabed, to a point directly under the buoy, needed to be covered with large rocks. A hopper barge ferried stones from a distant quarry to the worksite. The captain would spend some time getting perfectly aligned with the pipeline's direction, then "bombs away": the hull would split open along its length, the stones would drop out, freefall to the seabed and cover the pipe. Once the barge had left and visibility had cleared, we would dive to confirm that the drop was on target. The problem was the depth: we were running out of bottom time before the working day was over, and needed to hire one more diver to allow us to work a full day safely. Aberdeen HQ told us a guy was on his way. He would then take the oil company's small fixed-wing aircraft to Flotta the following day.

Lunchtime the next day found us all in the canteen when the new diver came in. He was a nice young guy from near Glasgow and was asked how he got on in Aberdeen the previous night. He got into a story of an amazing night, which started in a well-known bar. After meeting a rowdy, intoxicated group of female hairdressers, he was dragged to a nightclub called Fusion. He described in detail the woman who had begged him to follow her home, described the 4x4 car in the drive and even remembered the address, because he'd ordered a taxi the morning after. The car, house and hairdresser's wedding ring had all been paid for by the diver sitting beside me, who had been working with us for the past week. He said nothing, pushed his chair away from the table, packed his bag and left on the return flight of the same charter plane to Aberdeen. The young guy was quite affected by this revelation but she had worn no ring on the night out and he knew nothing of her marital status, so was blameless.

I only saw the other diver once after that. He had passed his saturation diving course, which was where the big money was, and was driving a soft-top 911 Porsche up Union Street in Aberdeen. Her loss.

Back in Aberdeen after the Flotta job, I got a call-out in Aberdeen harbour. This job was to teach me another lesson in prior planning and thinking outside the box for all possibilities that can go wrong before diving in murky water. The old fish dock was built in the late 1930s through to the early 1940s and the original metal piling was still in place. It was very worn and cracked in places. At high tide, this was allowing water to seep into the ground and into any void spaces behind the piling, under the building's foundations. As the tide dropped, it could not escape fast enough, causing the piles to buckle outward.

The underwater cutting equipment we used at the time was called Broco and consisted of an electrical tape-covered copper tube, holding thin mild steel rods like bicycle spokes and one magnesium spoke. This was inserted into a collet on a gun, with a thick welding cable leading to the generator running it. There was also a hose from a reducer on an oxygen bottle. A diver would fit a rod into the gun, say "Make it hot," and the supervisor on the surface would throw a heavy-duty switch to put electrical power into the rod. Once the rod was energised, the diver would touch the rod to the metal at the point to be burned, arc it and squeeze the gun's trigger lever to inject pure oxygen into the mix. As soon as it was cutting, the diver gave the order "make it cold" and the switch was flipped open. The rod would keep on self-burning at a savage 10,000 degrees. It was incredibly powerful.

The plan was to lower me in a basket with the Broco gear and I would burn a series of holes in the piles, to allow water to escape without buckling the piles any further. A dockyard crane was summoned and I clambered into the basket. I was handed the Broco gun and a quiver of burning rods and I told them over the helmet comms to lower me down. Once my head was underwater, everything went black in the silty water. I felt the basket bump the seabed and gave the "All Stop" command. Then I felt the piling with my fingers, cleaned some of the rust scale off and prepared to make my first cut. The supervisor flicked the switch to the closed position, and the electric buzz in my tooth fillings and around my head confirmed that the gun was live. I arced up and squeezed the oxygen trigger. The Broco rod sparked into life and burned straight through the old steel pile like butter.

Boom! The loudest underwater explosion I ever heard in my 22 years' commercial diving went off right in my face. I fell to my knees in the basket and I am sure that I blacked out for a second or two. My helmet's faceplate was cracked, and a stream of bubbles was pouring out from it.

"Up on the basket," I could feel myself speaking to the surface but I couldn't hear myself. My ears were still ringing from the blast.

Once I was deposited on the dockside like a dead fish, we worked out what had happened. There had always been a bad smell around the old fish dock area. Over the years, gas had escaped from the silt and rotten fish guts, and had built up under the dockside foundations, filling all of the small voids below. I had effectively lit the gas. Everyone felt the blast, including the crane driver high up in his cab.

Me cutting steel with Broco gear

RACING DAYS, RACING CRASHES

My addiction for fast bikes led me to try racing for a couple of years in 1987 and 1988. Well, that's not exactly true. There was one other small matter that influenced me. I had been banned from driving. It was my fault entirely. I had been at Knockhill racetrack watching the bike-racing and was heading home to Aberdeen. As I left Dundee, there was a long stretch of clear road and I opened the bike up. There were no other cars in front of me and the sun was behind me. It was perfect. As I got closer to Forfar, I began to see red brake lights and a tailback of traffic, so I slowed and crested a hill. As I squeezed past the stationary vehicles, I could make out two police cars with flashing blue lights, stopping all northbound traffic. I just knew they were waiting for me. The policemen waved me down to the front, held me there and then moved the two police cars off the road, allowing traffic to move. A third police car turned up behind us, and the occupants got out. I have never seen a policeman so angry. The driver's face was red as a beetroot and he tried to rip my helmet off without undoing the chinstrap. I held out my hand and asked him to calm down as I removed my helmet. His partner was standing behind him, slowly shaking his head from side to side at me, and put his finger to his lips in the universal "keep quiet" sign.

Beetroot face dragged me off the bike and threw me into the back of the police car, where I could clearly see on a digital display: 133.7mph. Oops.

I was taken to Forfar police station. After a few hours rotting in a cell, they charged me for speeding and let me go, to be sentenced to a year's ban a few months later. The bike was stolen a few weeks later, so with the insurance money, I bought new wheels and applied for a racing licence.

I loved the racing world and got some light sponsorship. But all of my money went into the black hole that racing any vehicle generates. My best result was eighth of 31 starters at a bumpy track near Edinburgh, though my favourite track was Knockhill in Fife. Tracy didn't really like racing but she came to watch one weekend. My friend and mechanic on the day, Roddy Hardie, had my Yamaha LC250 ready for my first race. Everything was looking good. I was on the third row of the grid and the track was wet, which I liked. The lights went green and my engine just died. No obvious reason; it just stopped. Everyone streaked past.

I managed to bump it into life and set off in last place. The race was 15 laps and I went nuts, growing horns trying to reel everyone in. By mid-race, I was about halfway through the pack of 30 starters. I was having a few slides on the wet track but nothing drastic, when all of a sudden, BANG! I lost the front end at a chicane and went down hard. I was behind the bike, face down and aquaplaning. I thought I had come to a stop but I remember looking up and seeing a shower of sparks in front of me as the side of the bike was ground away. My unplanned journey came to an end off the track.

I picked the dead bike up and pushed it to the barrier. Because I was entered in the next race with my big Honda CBR1000F, I needed to get my twisted LC250 and myself back to the pits as soon as possible. A van picked my bike up and transported us both back to my van. As I was getting onto the CBR, I was shouting to Roddy, "Did you warm it up?" Blood was running from the left arm of my leathers onto the white fuel tank of the big Honda. I had worn through the leather at the elbow and removed an area of skin. Adrenaline blocked any immediate pain. That would come later.

As I started it, prior to rushing down to the grid for the next race, I noticed Tracy staring at me. Her finger was pointing at her temple, saying, "You are f***ing mental."

My biggest and last crash was with a Suzuki GSXR750, a pure race bike. To cut a long story short, I got ready for the one qualifying run allowed on the hill climb that I had entered and beyond that, I don't remember anything else until I woke up in Aberdeen's Forester Hill Hospital. Apparently, I had howled up the first straight of the hill climb flat out, braked for the first corner and dropped the bike hard on oil dumped by the previous competitor. I had bowled up the road arms flailing and bounced through a mix of heather (good) and boulders (bad). When I came around, a nurse with a clipboard was ready to ask me some stupid (to me) questions:

"What's your name?"

"No idea."

"Date of birth?"

"No idea."

"What's the house or flat number in your address"?

"No idea, but I live above the Hawthorn bar." I had remembered the bar!

The extent of damage was a destroyed GSXR750, a broken collar bone, a lot of gravel rash and an egg-sized swelling on the back of my head, causing a big concussion that didn't let me remember anything for about 45 minutes after I woke up (apart from the bar, of course). I never got the helmet back because it had been split in the crash. Sean Marshall was there on the day with his girlfriend Lorna and apparently, I fell off right in front of them. For Lorna, the worst part of the whole ordeal was when they removed my racing boots in the ambulance and I had two completely different coloured socks on.

It came to the point after two seasons where I had to drop the racing. There was always going to be the possibility of a long layoff due to injury and when I was off work, I earned no money.

At one point, my Yamaha's two-stroke engine had a blown piston. Because I had no real workshop as such, I lugged it up three flights of stairs to my flat and laid newspapers out on the living-room floor while I stripped it. I had hoped to have it all done by the time Tracy got home from work. However, there are always complications. She wasn't best pleased.

Most problems involved in my crashes were down to two unavoidable factors – my seemingly possessed right throttle-hand and centrifugal force.

My trusty GSXR750 before I inadvertently "modified" it

A DRUNKEN TATTOO

After that crash, I was put on light duties at work for a while and I ended up as supervisor of a non-diving job west of Edinburgh in Grangemouth Docks, at the head of the Forth estuary. A vanload of Denso tape, drysuits and a caravan had been sent from Aberdeen to the worksite. The tape was to wrap and protect the splash zone between water and the air and to be fitted one metre below the surface and one metre above.

First, steel piles would be scraped of all marine growth and a layer of impregnated tape applied to each pile, followed by a heavy-duty layer of rubberised tape. The whole lot was secured with stainless steel banding. This arrangement extended the working life of a piling by 10 years for insurance purposes. The caravan was our changing room and tape storage room, and I was instructed to find a few labourers from the local area and pay them from a cash float I had been given.

So where do you go in an unfamiliar town to find labour?

The pub, of course!

I found the nearest bar and asked the barmaid if there was anyone looking for work. It wasn't long before I had four sorry-looking creatures presented to me as being "good to go by the way".

Next morning, I signed them in at the dockyard gate. The first job was instructing them on how to get in and out of a crushed neoprene drysuit. This was a lot harder than I had ever thought possible but I got them to the water's edge, only to be told that two of them couldn't swim. "No problem," I said. "You only need to float." The following hour was hilarious as I taught them to expel air from inside their suits. They were bobbing around, completely out of control, sometimes totally upside-down, trying to breathe the muddy contents of Grangemouth Docks. I called a break before instructing them on the ins and outs of actually taping the piles.

In a couple of days, they had cracked it. We would meet in the mornings, take the required amount of tape to the waterside and work through the morning. When lunchtime came, I paid for their bar lunch at various dodgy venues in the area – which was where my problems started.

In a local haunt, I was chatting to a barmaid with a mesmerising cleavage and finishing my haddock and chips, when I heard from somewhere behind me: "Psst, John." One of my workforce was peering round an exit door, frantically signalling for me to follow him, so I reluctantly paid up and left. Outside, he said, "Get in the car, quick!" We were using their dilapidated old Ford Granada as transport for the day, and I couldn't help noticing the giveaway lump of a Space Invaders machine sticking out of the boot. They had just robbed the pub of its machine! A quick visit to the seashore, a few blows from a crowbar and splash, the machine went to Davy Jones's locker (minus the coin contents, of course). We never went back to that bar.

The next day, once work was finished, they asked if I would stay back to sign them out of the dockyard a little later, as they had organised something with a dockyard worker. As I sat in the caravan, I started an inventory of the boxes of tape left and brewed a cup of tea. I heard the unmistakable sound of a clanking crane pull up outside but continued working on the tape count. After about 30 minutes of shouting and swearing, curiosity got the better of me and I stepped out... OMG! The Ford Granada was swinging around in mid-air. A railway sleeper had been passed through the open passenger and driver windows, and hooked up to the crane. The car had been lifted off the ground by the roof and they were all happily walking underneath it, changing a knackered exhaust pipe for one that they had no doubt "found" the previous night. I stepped back into the caravan and closed my eyes.

This job lasted a few weeks, and one Friday, I said, "Goodbye, see you all on Monday." I knew they were tied in with a dodgy solicitor. He would get the job of cleaning out the houses of people who had died with no relatives and would sell the contents at auction. As far as I could gather, any items of value never reached the auction. Monday morning came around and as we were suiting up, prior to walking down to the water, I could see that one of the guys was in pain. "What's wrong?" I asked.

"Er, we were clearing a house and we found a tattoo kit, so Jimmy here tattooed my back."

"Let's have a look."

He took his shirt off and turned around. I was speechless. He had asked Jimmy for a thistle in the centre of his back with "Scotland the Brave" around it, though what I was looking at had no words to describe it.

They thought that to avoid any unnecessary pain, they should drink a large quantity of whisky first. This included Jimmy the needle man, so off they went on a serious session. Jimmy, who had never even held a tattoo needle in his life, eventually decided that they were suitably drunk and the show began.

The thistle was first. It was straight out of a three-year-old's crayon book. This was topped by lettering that was equally crap, if not worse. The last sweep of the word "Brave" skirted out to the side with a final flourish, but that was it. Job done.

The tattooed guy painfully levered himself off the table and stood up. Everyone's jaw dropped. Jimmy had been standing at his head as his victim lay flat out, and he had drawn the whole abysmal effort upside down!

My last incident with these guys was just a couple of hours from my final departure. We were packing to leave and I was in the water with three of them, finishing off. I had sent one to clean the caravan, prior to it being towed back to Aberdeen. I could faintly make out sirens in the distance, and as we were in the middle of a gas plant, I hoped it wasn't anything serious. The sirens got louder and louder until I thought I better take a look for our own safety. I swam to the dockside and climbed out.

Horror! The idiot I had given the job of cleaning the caravan to had taken all the empty cardboard boxes that had held the tape, made a big pile and then set fire to it. This was right next to a massive onion-shaped LPG gas tank, and the fire brigade were in full-action mode, hosing everything down.

I can't remember how I managed to wriggle out of that one, but it was a massive relief when I had the Grangemouth sign in my rear-view mirror for the last time.

REVENGE ON THE SNARLING DOG

Once again, I was offered a job in Saudi Arabia, but this time in the Red Sea and south of Jeddah. I met the rest of the dive team in Dhahran for briefing.

Basically, a desalination plant in a very remote area was run on oil from Sudan. The usual rusty, decrepit tanker for transporting the cargo had misjudged its berthing and crashed into one of the massive jetties (or dolphins) that the tanker was supposed to tie alongside for the oil offload. A 400-ton lump of concrete had been knocked off the legs of the dolphin, so we had the job of making it all good again.

On our first night in Jeddah in our crumbling hotel, we watched as on TV, 17 men were shown lined up with hessian bags on their heads. It turned out that these were the next day's recipients of the ever-busy "execution by sword". They were paraded on TV all evening until we turned in, prior to the dusty morning trip south.

We set off early and were seeing signs for Mecca along the highway. I was looking forward to a glimpse of the place but it was not to be. Before you get anywhere near the city, a sign strung over the highway stated: "No non-Muslims beyond this point." We had to take a side road, and looking back to the highway, I could see religious police stationed to check if Johnny Infidel was trying to sneak through.

We made our way to the desalination plant and were put up in what had been a large Japanese working camp. The whole show had been built by Mitsubishi Heavy Industries. A nice couple of Japanese men introduced themselves as Mr Nishimoto and Mr Watanabe – I've no idea how I have remembered their names after so many years, but they were real characters. They paid our Filipino divers a few rials to do the usual Japanese morning exercise with them as the divers were not interested in doing anything unless they were paid. The divers were soon brewing

71

their own alcohol and were a sorry sight in the mornings but 10 out of 10 to them: they arrived every morning for the small amount of money given in exchange for the pitiful exercise attempt.

The job was slow work. So much preparation had to be done before pouring concrete for the new massive slab. The legs had to be reinforced and a massive hole dug in the seabed to pour a slab of concrete at seabed level to tie the legs together. We were using what's best described as an extremely effective underwater vacuum cleaner called an airlift at this point. It was a long and dangerous 24in-diameter steel pipe, hanging off the crane. The bottom "divers' end" had a quarter-turn air valve with a low-pressure hose leading to a road compressor. Air was injected into the pipe when a diver turned the valve, then ran up the inside, expanding all the way to the surface. Due to the Venturi effect, this dragged everything off the seabed and up the pipe. If a diver was not careful and was in the wrong place, his helmet could be easily ripped off his head, or as Welshman Bill Evans found out, seriously bruised plums because a leg fitted perfectly up the pipe.

I was down with the 24in airlift dangling off the crane, sucking the seabed up, when I uncovered an industrial hard hat with Japanese writing on the front. I set it to one side and at the end of the dive, brought it with me to the surface. I found a welding rod, some feathers and duct tape, and fashioned an arrow on each side of the hat for fun. I'll never forget the look on Mr Nishimoto's face when he saw it. At the beginning of the contract, a construction barge was moored there and Mr Nishimoto's friend had been washed off in bad weather and died. That was his hat. Oops.

The job progressed well. The mooring dolphin was back to looking as it should and there was only a clean-up job to do. Most of the expat divers were taken over to the Gulf side of Saudi, but Bill Evans and I were left to finish it off with the Filipinos.

We were both still living on the Japanese camp but the Filipinos were in their own labour camp. They had cockfighting, video hire and alcohol brewing going on, among other dodgy businesses, so every now and then, I would squeeze through a gap in the link fence. The problem was that there was a certain white collie-sized desert dog living in the Filipino camp, and it hated white men. It would constantly rush in and try to bite my feet and ankles. No matter how quiet I was, he would be there with teeth showing.

On my birthday, I was invited to a party in my honour. I squeezed through the fence and walked to the makeshift community hall that the divers had built. They produced their home-made alcohol. Everything was going great, with many stories being swapped. My divers were, almost to a man, former Filipino SEALs, trained by the US and very competent. They had a million stories of fighting the Muslim rebels in Mindanao and other locations around their country.

Platters of food were brought in and spread over the long table that we shared. The Filipino tradition while drinking is to have snacks (much like peanuts and crisps in the west). However, their style is small snacks of mostly different cooked meats, innards and fish. They call it pulutan. I was offered a weird-looking sample, and as I have never been squeamish with food, I popped a piece into my mouth. It looked like a tube with a green filling, and turned out to be boiled cow's intestine stuffed with some unknown vegetable. But it was really tasty. Next came some pieces of white meat covered in a thick sweet brown sauce. This too tasted delicious, so I had a couple more pieces. I could see the guys all trying to hold back their laughter, so I said, "Go on then, what's the joke?"

The reply was totally unexpected. "This is the dog that always tried to bite you, sir!"

That explained why I hadn't been accosted at the fence gap in the fence on my way to the party. I felt sorry for him, but I couldn't bring him back. So I asked for another bit.

LOCKED UP IN A BANGKOK JAIL

Tracy and I decided on Thailand as a holiday destination after that Red Sea contract, so we timed my leave date to meet in Bangkok.

We booked a hotel in the capital close to Nana Plaza. We decided to stay close to the hotel for the first night, so we went out and tried some street food. I love Thai food and after the meal, we started on a mini-pub crawl. I had spent 90 dry days in Saudi, so my drinking head was definitely not calibrated. It didn't take too long before I was feeling the effects.

We wound up going from one girly bar to another with all kinds of weird and wonderful happenings on show. The last drinking venue of the evening was the Hog's Head bar, owned by a Canadian guy and his Thai wife. He was larger than life and trying to get as much alcohol into us as possible. Tracy had sensibly stopped at that point, but being stupid, I followed the Canadian's recommendation and started on the Mekong whisky. Only 33 different chemicals in it, I learned later.

I woke up in a noisy room, packed inside a small, padlocked, tack-welded rebar cage. My mouth felt like the bottom of Sitting Bull's wampum bag and I had a banging headache. I had somehow lost my flip-flops and my feet had been feasted on by mosquitoes. They looked like two pink inflated surgical gloves.

I remember saying out loud, "Where the f**ck am I?"

As everything swam into focus, I tried to piece the evening together: food, Tracy, bars, boobs, Canadian, then the last memory... Mekong whisky.

Outside my cage, I saw the back of what appeared to be a chubby policeman sitting at a desk reading a newspaper. A dark tuk-tuk-filled busy street was beyond him, the front of the building completely open. I realised that I must have been arrested. But for what?

I couldn't remember. I checked my hands quickly: no cuts nor abrasions, no tender spots on my face so hopefully, no fighting had taken place. The cage was "Thai size", so I couldn't sit up straight. My head was bent at an angle and when I called out to the policeman, "Excuse me," he turned around, looked at me then went back to his newspaper.

"Excuse me," I said more loudly.

With an audible sigh, he folded his newspaper and carefully laid it on the desk, pushed his chair away and walked over to me. "You drink too much, mista." I immediately agreed and did what I have always done if any contact with the police happened my way: I became Mr Nice Guy.

I apologised for anything that had happened and gradually got to the root of my heinous crime. I had ended up having an argument with Tracy, so she had left the bar. I had then drunk more of the free-flowing Mekong whisky until I fell asleep, leaning on my arms on the bar. The Canadian eventually managed to wake me up and presented me with my bar bill. There was a slight problem: Tracy had all of our money.

So, being the good bloke that he wasn't, he called the Thai Old Bill, who carted me off in a riot tuk-tuk. And now here I was, sitting in a cage like a mosquito-bitten *Apocalypse Now* extra.

The policeman had livened up a little by this point, so I tried to make light of the situation. At one point I got him to laugh, and pointing at the revolver hanging off his belt, I said, "That's a very big gun you have." This was obviously his pride and joy. Quick as a flash he drew it, opened the chamber and poured out the fat rounds into his free hand.

His next move was bizarre, but it would become even crazier a few minutes later. He passed the empty pistol through the bars to me. I took it, and opened and closed the chamber a few times, stroking his pride by telling him that this was a real man's weapon... blah, blah. I asked him the calibre and he said the immortal words: ".357 Magnum."

I directly said, "Clint Eastwood, Dirty Harry."

He knew exactly what I meant and was loving the conversation. "Crint Eastwoo, me Crint Eastwoo, make my day." At that point, he took one of the rounds, held it up, showed me the .357 stamp on the bottom and passed it through the bars.

So here I am, sitting in a cage in a Thai holding cell with an unarmed policeman in front of me, a .357 Magnum in one hand and a live round to fit it in the other. I quickly did what any sane person would do: I gave them back. I then cracked the million-dollar question: "What are you going to do with me?" He turned around and ominously walked out.

Ten minutes later, he returned with his police jacket and hat on, squatted down in front of my cage and asked, "You take me drinking? You pay?" I would have agreed to anything at that point to escape the cage. Well, maybe not anything, but you get the idea.

He produced a padlock key, opened the cage and we got in his police car: no paperwork, nothing. We shot through the dark backstreets of Bangkok. It was around 04.00 when we screeched to a halt outside of a block of ghetto apartments and he told me to follow him. We climbed some filthy stairs until he let himself into one of the doors. He pointed at the sofa, so I sat down in his apartment, which resembled the inside of a laundry. It was full of folded clothes! He came back into the room wearing a pair of jeans and a T-shirt and gestured that we should leave.

Back in the car, I broke the bad news that I had no money, which is why I was in this position in the first place. He said, "Which hotel you live in? We go get your money." We shot off again at breakneck speed. At the hotel, as soon as I walked past the reception with the policeman two steps behind, I could see my room key was missing from the numbered shelf behind the receptionist, so I knew Tracy was in the room. I continued to the lift and went up to my floor, still racking my brains how to get out of the situation. I knew she was in the room and would be in a deep sleep as she would have been exhausted from the flight, but was also pretty inebriated. I knocked lightly: no answer. I knocked again but got the same lack of response. At that point, I sat down in the corridor and told him she was a very deep sleeper and wore earplugs, so I would have to sit here until morning. He looked at me in disgust, threw his two hands towards me and made for the lift.

I ran down the stairs and watched him get into his car and drive off. My next move was finding a friendly room cleaner and getting her to open my door for me. Tracy, totally unaware of my mad night, was rudely awoken and in a total daze, made to pack up at lightning speed and check out.

We lived together for five years in the Aberdeen flat until she met a plumber or joiner.

I welcomed my new-found freedom and moved on.

WATCHING OUT FOR MINES

With one phone call, I got back in touch with my old Saudi diving company Algosaibi and headed east to pick up the usual 90-day trips again. We were working on a fleet of diving support vessels when the Iraqi sabre rattling started and Saddam's invasion force burst into Kuwait on August 2, 1990. By mid-January 1991, the first Gulf War was beginning with allied air strikes and by February 25, 1991, Kuwait was liberated. During this time, my ship was still working in the northern Saudi waters. We were by now seeing a lot of wreckage from the war to the north of us. We found a bullet-riddled lifeboat and other wreckage floating down the Gulf and were also shelled at one point, so we decided to head out to deeper waters and safety.

Our biggest worry was the large number of buoyant mines that had been released by the Iraqi Navy with no mooring systems. They were just released to float freely around the Gulf until a vessel or a platform contacted one of the horns.

Some bright spark decided that we should lay a series of large concrete anchors with buoys around all of the platforms, and stretch fishing gillnets between them to stop the mines. So we loaded up with equipment, steamed north and began laying everything out. Once all our anchors and nets were set, we left the gear to soak for a couple of days, then took a large inflatable boat supplied with the equipment and lifted the net onto the boat's bow, so that the net ran up onto the front and off the back. I basically drove the boat along the net while the guys cleaned the dead marine creatures out of it. In no time, we were all hurting from a multitude of jellyfish stings and fish fin punctures. The funniest incident was when Steve Leaney, a guy who wasn't shy of a bit of drama, got very aerated on the bow of the inflatable boat, shouting ever more loudly in a croaky voice, "Shark, shark, SHARK." I was driving the boat and didn't hear him at first, but when the shark started coming over the bow with its long, snaggly teeth snapping, I backed off as quickly as I could. We managed to unwrap the big fish, so that one had lady luck on its side and swam away to freedom. Many more didn't.

Soon after we started this programme, we spotted a three-horned mine floating close to the ship. I convinced Steve to come with me to mark its location with a small buoy and anchor, because darkness was approaching and the mine was only just buoyant. At times, it would disappear below the waves before popping back up in a different position. A Saudi explosive ordinance disposal team had been called, but we needed the buoy and anchor as a point of reference if darkness arrived and we lost sight of the mine.

I loaded the anchor and buoy/rope into the inflatable and Steve jumped in. I told him in front of everyone that as I was a former clearance diver, an old trick we used in the Navy was to sit on the rubber inflatable tube so that if the mine exploded, he would be cushioned from the blast. He somehow believed me, and perched on that wobbly tube like he was glued to it. Everyone was howling with laughter while watching him through binoculars from our dive vessel until I got close enough to the mine and marked it. It was an Italian mine and had been confirmed as contact-only: no magnetic or acoustic methods of initiation.

A free floating buoyant contact mine close to my ship, with Saudi Arabian oil installations in the background

The Saudi Navy eventually turned up and set up their gear on the back deck. This had been my job in the Navy, so I was obviously interested in their kit and methods. My take can be summed up in one word: diabolical. They were cutting detonating cord on a steel deck using a steel flick knife with a detonator attached. (Static electricity would have been enough to initiate the electrical detonator they were using.) Then, for some unknown reason, the guy in charge lifted the detonator up and flicked it with his finger and thumb. That was it. I removed myself from the back deck very rapidly and sat on the bow behind the anchor winch, until they assembled the charges and left.

I heard that they loaded their charges "live" into the inflatable before pounding over the choppy sea to the mine. First attempt was a misfire, and instead of waiting a set amount of time before returning, they went straight back in and set another charge on it. This time, Boom! A nice Roman candle lit up the sky: job done. I would guess that those guys are not around today if that was their usual modus operandi.

Shortly after this, we were called further south because Saddam had opened the floodgates in Kuwait, releasing an ocean of crude oil into the Persian Gulf. We could smell it coming before we saw it. Desalination plants, which suck in a huge amount of seawater and turn it into fresh, were an obvious problem. We had shipping containers of oil booms on the beach close to our first attempt at protecting a desalination plant. However, once the booms were deployed and the oil arrived, it steamrollered straight over the booms. Everything had to be shut down.

The oil was like thick tar, not the runny oil that we are used to in our car engines. It was about a metre thick and had a lot of marine life stuck in it: birds, turtles, dolphins, whales. Nothing could escape the toxic mess. At one point, we were very close to sucking the foul tarry mess into the ship's main engine intakes but managed to move slowly offshore and find an area where it was less dense.

It took a very long time for this oil to disappear. In the end, it ended up rolling around on the seabed like sand-covered tar balls, before somehow being absorbed back into the earth. There is no sign of this disaster today.

I had the chance to take a long-term diving job in Abu Dhabi at this point, so I sold my Aberdeen flat, upped sticks, bailed out of the UK and rented a flat in the sun.

A MAXIMUM-SECURITY PRISON

My delight at living in the sun was short-lived. After an afternoon with a couple of lads in a watering hole called Jukebox Junction, we changed venue. We'd been on the "buy one jug, get one free" margaritas all afternoon and were babbling as we got out of the taxi at the new drinking hole. To cut a long story short, I was crossing the main street with Kevin Blowes in the centre of town, which is like a six-lane racetrack. Suddenly a crazy Arab ran a red light and ran me over. My head went through the windscreen and my left elbow was gashed to the bone, as it removed the wing mirror. The worst was yet to come. As he collided with me, his bumper shattered my lower left leg. My tibia and fibula were smashed to pieces.

I woke up in a zoo – or that's how it felt! Strange people were staring at me as I lay there in a daze. I was in the Abu Dhabi general hospital. My company quickly arranged to get me out and transferred me to a private hospital later that day. I was booked for an operation but I had to wait for the swelling to go down on my lower leg before Dr Sharif, an Iraqi doctor, could take a peek inside.

Complete with crutches, a plaster cast and two steel plates, I was released a month after my arrival to recuperate in the company staff house. A couple of days passed before I was suddenly summoned to the police station to get my passport back. In Arab countries, it's the first thing they take to stop you fleeing the country. I hobbled into the station and was guided along a corridor, through a steel-barred door... and clang! I was locked up.

One week later, after sleeping on the hard tile floor, I found myself in front of a judge with the Arab driver. Basically, the judge told the Arab that he'd been a very bad boy and had to pay me 12,000 dirhams, which is just over £2000. He seemed happy about this, got his passport back and flew out to Lebanon that night without coughing up a penny, never to be seen again.

I was on those crutches for 13 months and living off the profit from my flat in Aberdeen. I finally got my diving medical back, then pulled a regular diving job with a seaborne part of the Abu Dhabi government where I stayed for over six years. During this time, while I was on holiday in the Algarve, I met my wife Catrin who is Swedish, and shortly after, I moved to Stockholm with everything I owned: a Yamaha YZF750SP and a rucksack.

I was still working for the Abu Dhabi Petroleum Ports Operating Company – part of the Abu Dhabi government – at this point. I was heading back to work from Sweden to take over as diving supervisor on board the old diving vessel *Ahmed* and had a night in Abu Dhabi. The guy I was taking over from was a former Royal Marine, John Alden, who had a dream trip to Australia booked. He'd be living on a vessel on the Great Barrier Reef for his leave and diving with all manner of exotic fish. What could go wrong?

I dropped my bag off in my East European-staffed hotel and headed across town, opened the door to an Irish bar that I'd frequented when I lived in Abu Dhabi and immediately bumped into a group of people I hadn't seen for four years. The beer and banter were flowing, but I realised that I had an early cut-off time because I had a helicopter to catch at 06.30 to relieve John and get him on his way to Australia. I left the bar at 23.30 and took a cab across town, went into the foyer, and the Russian receptionist handed me my key. I remember the room number 84 to this day. It was room four on floor eight.

As I got into the lift, I pressed what I thought was my floor button. The doors started to close but two little brown hands were thrust through the gap and they opened again. A Pakistani man got in and pressed his button. As he pressed it, I realised that he pushed the eighth-floor button and I had earlier pressed the seventh by mistake. We rode up quickly to the seventh floor. The doors opened, closed and we headed for floor eight. He went mental! "Why you press floor seven, waste my time?" etc.

I told him no uncertain terms to Foxtrot Oscar.

"You swear at me? You swear at me?"

"Listen, mate. If you don't f**ck off, I'll do more than swear at you."

"You threaten me?"

So I backhanded him once across the ear and went to my room.

I put CNN on the TV and made a cup of coffee while I sorted my bag for the trip to the heliport in a few hours.

There was a knock at the door.

I opened it to half of Abu Dhabi's constabulary. They cuffed me, ankles and hands, and dragged me to a riot wagon. We made a dash across town to the hospital and a blood test. Yup, there was alcohol in my blood. What a surprise.

I was kept for two days in an underground holding cell. The company eventually tracked me down and sent a bloke from the office to see me. It wasn't looking good!

On the morning of the third day, there was a loud clattering of keys and the steel door swung open, I was bundled into to a barred wagon and driven to a maximum-security prison in the desert. On the way, the scrawny Afghan prisoners in the back of the wagon peeled off a bit of plywood laminate. Quick as you like, they had picked the locks on their handcuffs and sat like nothing was wrong, hands behind their heads, just enjoying the ride. They offered me the same treatment but I declined. I thought I was in enough trouble at that point.

I knew when we were getting close to the prison because I could smell human shit. We drove up to a massive metal portcullis in the prison wall. It lifted to allow us entry, then ominously slammed shut.

I gave up all my possessions in a dingy room and climbed into a blue prison suit with a badge pinned to the chest. It had Arabic writing on it, which I later found out stated my crime – Boxing! A pair of surly guards escorted me to my new residence, a stifling eight-man room on the middle floor of three, with 36 men living in it. I settled in for my first night.

For some strange reason, I was given one of the eight concrete plinths that were the "beds", but as darkness approached on my first night of incarceration, a queue was ominously forming up outside my door. Fearing the worst (there were 220 men on my floor and I was the only white boy), I went to the door to face down the crowd. Just as I got there, a section of green garden hose threaded its way down on the outside of the bars from the floor above. The first bloke in the queue, who happened to be an Indian, stepped forward, stretched his hand through the bars and grabbed the pipe, he then put it to his mouth and in a stream of rapid-fire Hindi, he shouted something up it. Once finished, he put it to his ear to receive his reply. It was the prison telephone, and they were all queuing for their turn to talk to their mates upstairs.

I met some real characters there. I felt sorry for some who should not have been anywhere near a prison. One old Qatari man was a raging alcoholic and slept in the corridor every night on the tiles, fighting his demons. After being found face-down in an alcoholic stupor in an Abu Dhabi public park, he was hauled to court and the judge had passed sentence. "When you can recite the full Koran to me, you will be released." This old boy couldn't string a drooling sentence together, let alone a full book. For sure, he'd spend the rest of his life in there.

Another one was an Indian guy who was driving to work. A police car was behind him and he was listening to music on the radio and "car dancing" – as most people do but never admit. Indian people are known far and wide to wobble their heads around. This is exactly what he was doing to a bit of Bhangra music, bothering no-one and just enjoying another sunny morning on the way to work. Suddenly, he was pulled over, dragged to court and charged with the heinous crime of (direct translation from Arabic) "driving while not keeping your head on your shoulders". He was handed a three-month sentence!

A bloke who had involuntarily farted in a supermarket while bending down to pick up a rice cooker was reported to security – three months for air pollution!!

The saddest one was a 21-year-old Yemeni guy. He was 14 when his father stabbed his uncle to death. His father told him to take the blame because they wouldn't jail a 14-year-old. Wrong: he had a death sentence over his head and his father had bailed out to Birmingham in the UK, leaving his son behind to face the ultimate sentence.

For every person held in that prison, the police force received 100 dirhams per day from Sheik Zayed, the big boss. The more you catch, the more money is in the pot. I can't say if this system is still in place, but I wouldn't be surprised. So beware: when things go wrong in the Emirates, they go wrong very quickly and there's no stopping it.

One Chinese lad who spoke almost no English managed to get me to understand his story over a couple of days with drawings and arm gestures. He was fresh in from China and he and his brother were being driven at night from the airport to a construction site, when a large truck executed a U-turn on the highway. The Chinese guy had been lying across the back seat trying to catch a little sleep, but his brother and the driver were decapitated as the car drove under the trailer. The Arabic tag on his prison suit said "Drinking". He explained through sign language that he was a marathon runner and never drank a drop. He was awaiting sentence.

The inmates' ingenuity never ceased to amaze me. They mixed Arabic bread with tea to make glue to stick things on the walls. They mixed bread with water, which was formed into tubes and dried in the sun between the bars. Once the tubes were fully hardened, a little Filipino who possessed a small blade that had been smuggled in carved the most exquisite chess pieces you can imagine.

One night, I could hear singing and a tune was being played. I followed the music and found a group of guys with a homemade guitar. The body had been fashioned from cardboard boxes and water into a papier-mâché mix; laminates of plywood had been removed from the back of the two toilet doors to make the fretboard and somehow, they had acquired fishing line for the strings. The lad operating the contraption would never be a threat to Jimmy Hendrix but he did brilliantly with what he had.

During my time there, I studied the routines. I found a way out: no digging holes or knocking down walls. I know that if I had been a lifer, I could have escaped that prison. It only needed one or two prisoners to assist.

The food was dire. I am not squeamish but when there are living creatures moving around in your meal, it has a tendency to affect your appetite. Ten days later when I was released, I was 10kg lighter.

Every morning, Arabic guards would stick a sheet of paper on a wall to show who was to be taken to court that day. I can't read the language, so I just quickly checked for my name on the list and finally picked it out after nine days. I was taken to court that afternoon in another caged wagon.

As I waited my turn to go into court, all the Afghan and Indian prisoners had a representative from their respective embassies turn up, so I was waiting for a caped crusader to turn up from mine. However, as the queue became shorter, I realised I was on my own for this appearance. I heard that during my time inside, the British Embassy had been informed but thought it best not to get involved. They are a useless shower that I have had the displeasure of dealing with in various corners of the world. They are the offspring of a wealthy section of society that seems to treat their position as a way to run a private and exclusive gentleman's club at the taxpayers' expense.

I was quickly given my sentence of 1000 dirhams. However, as the prison had been paid 100 dirhams every day for my stay, it was considered "time served" and I was to be officially released the next day. When I was being prepared for my release, I wrote down a number that the Chinese runner managed to give me by sign language and finger counting, then rolled it into a thin paper pin. I held it tight between my fingers as I was frisked before getting my clothes and possessions back. Once out, I unrolled the paper and called the number. I told the person on the other end the story of the Chinese kid. He said in a heavy Asian accent that he was aware of the problem and he was to be released in the next couple of days, and that if I went to a certain Chinese restaurant in town, I would get a free meal. I contemplated it but in the end, I never went.

I was taken to the Novotel in the middle of Abu Dhabi by a company driver and given a room. I was told to wait there because an expat from the company (my boss) was to visit me. I obviously thought I would be fired. However, he told me, "I am supposed to give you a serious bollocking, so consider it done. Now, tell me all about it."

Most work at this time (when I wasn't in an Arab jail) involved hooking tankers up to large buoys and connecting the relevant hoses to allow the tanker to fill up with crude oil, close to Zirku Island. When the buoys were free of tankers, we would carry out subsea maintenance on all of the valves and so on that controlled the system. One of the biggest jobs that periodically came our way was changing out one of the enormous buoys that the crude oil tankers were moored to. These are huge. Each had eight chains holding them in position and each link of chain weighed 127kg. The company vessel dedicated to this task was an old crane ship, the MV *Barracuda*, captained by a garlic sausage-munching German called Dieter. He had a crazy Filipino crew. One, who was the crane driver, had an obsession for swords and was actually making them on board. Zorro got pissed up at Christmas and the terrified crew locked themselves inside the mess to escape his sword-swinging threats. The door turned out to be no match for his swordsmanship, so he chopped it up then entered the room. The crew were cornered and with no escape route, they had no other option than to rush and overpower him. Another day in paradise!

Persian Gulf pre-dive with a Kirby 17

PRACTICAL JOKES

On one of these buoy changes, I was working with Mark Jones. He'd been an army Royal Engineer in a past life. He was a great practical joker. Nothing was safe, from finding your boots nailed to the wooden deck after a coffee break to food dye in the shower nozzle. Anything could happen – and did.

After too many pranks at our expense, we hatched a revenge plan. When he came up from his dive covered in crude oil, after a particularly messy subsea hose change, he leaped in the shower with a pot of Swarfega to clean himself up. He'd left his clean clothes on the handrail outside the shower compartment, so Nick Needham (RIP), the diving supervisor, grabbed his underpants and ran into the galley. We got the hottest chillies known to man, rubbed them into the crotch area and replaced them on the handrail with his kit.

We broke for lunch and were enjoying the cook's weekly curry and rice when a dishevelled Mark staggered into the mess looking extremely distressed,

"John, I have a problem."

"What is it?"

"Can Swarfega affect your skin?"

"Why?"

"Cos my f***ing knackers are on fire!"

We all collapsed in fits of laughter.

It was on the MV *Barracuda* during another subsea hose change that a strange thing happened. The tide was running strongly, so from a safety aspect, all diving operations had ceased. The sea was flat calm and the sun was beating down, and we were about to go off deck, when Mark said, "What's that?" He pointed at a small splashing shape drifting quickly towards us. It looked as if it would come right down our starboard side, so Mark said, "Grab my feet."

I hung him over the side and as the small shape drifted past, he grabbed a cat by the scruff of the neck. It landed on the wooden deck and didn't move, so we picked it up with heavy welding gloves (rabies possibility) and took it to some shade. We got some water and left it to its own devices. A lot of its hair had fallen out due to being in the sea for so long, but it pulled round and after getting a tin of sardines every morning, it wasn't long before it was purring around the ship, thinking it was Top Cat. Who knows how it got there? Probably thrown overboard from a ship somewhere in the Gulf.

The next time we berthed in Abu Dhabi, it left the ship and was last seen running around the dockside, bald as a coot, chasing girl cats.

Over one extended period of time, Mark was having a running joke with the guy who did his job when he was not there (the job was 4 weeks on, 4 weeks off).

I entered the Das Island harbour diving office once day and found it in total darkness. Mark was crouched at the window. "Get down, get down," he hissed. He had a piece of string running through the cracked window, to a cardboard fruit box with a stick propping it up, and a slice of bread under it in the shade. The string was tied to the stick and he was waiting for a seagull to go under, to pull the string and catch it! I got bored and left him to it.

The next day, his relief arrived on the plane. They did a quick handover at the small airport terminal and the incoming guy went to change into his overalls, prior to meeting the superintendent to discuss the workload for the month ahead.

He dropped his bags and did a quick sweep of the room, as he knew Mark could set something up. Nothing. So he opened his wardrobe to get his overalls and bang! He was hit full in the face by an extremely angry shitehawk the size of an albatross. It was trying to take off in the confines of the room and destroying everything with its frantic flapping. Eventually, the door was opened and it burst out, but it had left some rather large green-

and-yellow stinking fishy deposits in the wardrobe, where it had been incarcerated all night.

On Mark's return, the incident was never mentioned and the usual handover in the airport terminal took place. The room key was ceremoniously handed over and the plane left.

Mark opened the door gingerly and looked around the room. Nothing. He opened the wardrobe door slowly. Nothing. As time was pressing for his meeting with the superintendent, he went to his overall shelf in the wardrobe. "That's strange," he muttered, because only one pair of blue company overalls were on the shelf. He dragged them out, unfolded them and found that they had been "adapted". His relief had visited the island's resident Indian tailor and customised them with bright-red clown pockets over the blue material and best of all, massive Elvis flares with a red flash. Mark actually put them on and went to the meeting.

During a stint for another diving company in Abu Dhabi, an Indian accountant, "Sheik", saw an April fool joke played out by the general manager. A year later, the staff house cook turned up in the general manager's office, bawling his eyes out. "Sir, I got a call from your office and my father has died. I don't know what to do. I need a ticket to fly home and my salary is not due until two weeks." By now, the poor chap was almost on his knees, with tears running down his cheeks.

The manager sympathised, then reached for the phone to call Sheik to sort the salary. But suddenly, he noticed Sheik standing in the office doorway, picking his teeth with a toothpick, and through a beaming smile Sheikh shouted, "April fool!" The joke was somehow lost in translation, and the poor cook caught a taxi back to the staff house, trying to work out how his father was still alive!

Whenever really bad weather arrived offshore, we headed into Abu Dhabi for shelter. The dive vessels could take on food, fuel and water and the lads were let loose on the drinking haunts throughout the city. One of the favourites was the Irish bar I mentioned earlier. One evening, after about 10 pints, John Alden decided he wanted to have his ear pierced. A stud was found from who knows where and I was put in charge of the operation. I pushed as hard as I could on his left ear lobe and somehow managed to stab the blunt stub through. I then squeezed the clip on the back and as far as I knew, that was that. We carried on drinking and eventually staggered back to the ship. Next morning, John was in agony. His ear had swollen to an abnormal size and was beetroot red. On closer inspection, I had pushed the clip on far too tightly. It was pulled out, cleaned up and I believe it healed quickly.

BITTEN BY A FISH

The bad weather cleared and we headed back offshore. My ship went to the Zirku Island area, then tied up to a small platform that was used as a radio repeater station. Signals were received and amplified by electronic gadgetry to the surrounding area. The waters around this platform teemed with aquatic life. It was a restricted area, and vessels seldom visited, so while the lads were inside having lunch, I flipped a scuba set on my back, grabbed a spear gun and climbed down the dive ladder.

It was like being in a massive personal aquarium. I watched huge numbers of fish swimming around the platform and waited for a big school of jack to swim past. I took aim at one big fish and let the spear go, hitting the fish just behind the gills. It just stopped, stone dead, trailing a green plume as it sank, impaled on my spear (due to the water filtering the light, blood comes out green underwater, not red).

I pulled the fish in and using a welding rod attached to a thin cord, I threaded the rod through its mouth and out of its gills. This was how we collected all of our spear-caught fish underwater. I wound the cord around my left hand, so the fish's head was close to my hand, and reloaded the spear gun. It wasn't long before a school of barracuda came gliding along. I was holding my left arm through the dive ladder and stretched out for balance, taking aim with my right hand at a respectable-sized fish when I noticed a small one turn head-on to me. It hung there for a second, then accelerated. Bang! It hit me at full speed on my left wrist. The barracuda then froze for some unexplained reason. I prised it off my arm and the fish then came back to life and swam off. It was now my turn to leak green stuff and underwater, it seemed to be quite a lot. I climbed the ladder and found the medical box, washed the wound on my wrist with surgical spirit and bound it with a bandage. Slowly, over the next hour or so, I was experiencing numbness in my thumb. Luckily our next stop was the nearby island of Zirku, so I

94

found a doctor and was diagnosed with carpal tunnel syndrome! The fish's teeth had affected a nerve. This numbness lasted for around four months, but I still have scars from the top two front teeth to this day. I can only surmise that the small barracuda saw my shiny chrome Casio G-shock watch buckle, with the dead fish's nose close to it, and thought it was food. The bottom teeth actually hit the buckle and only the top two (the biggest) had cut into my wrist. A centimetre lower and it would have hit an artery.

A FAKE MARINE

I eventually quit Abu Dhabi Petroleum Ports Authority after six and a half years and found myself working for CCC once again, from an old beaten-up vessel called the *Conco III*. We were trying to do pipeline surveys in shamal season. A shamal is a strong wind that blows down the Persian Gulf and for some strange reason, normally blows for three days or five. During one of these shamals, we ended up anchored for shelter behind Das Island, a small island oil refinery with a runway and accommodation for workers.

It was coming up to lunchtime on board and I overheard a "thick northern git", whom I'll just call Dixon, gobbing off about weapons in the military to someone who had never served. I overheard this and it immediately raised my suspicions about something I had suspected for a while: he was talking crap. This would normally not be much of a problem, but he was professing to be a former Royal Marine, which looked extremely doubtful and seriously irritated me.

That evening, the weather blew up so bad that we took shelter in the small island harbour. Because I had worked there in the past, I jumped off the vessel and located John Farrell, my old boss who had served in the Special Boat Service in a past life. I explained about Dixon and he said, "Invite the lads up to the sailing club after scran, and we'll have a laugh." I went back to the ship and told the lads that we were all off to the sailing club for a pint.

An hour or so later, the whole company were fed, in good spirits and heading up the jetty for some frosty refreshment. At this point, I should explain about clubs and Das Island at that time. Basically, if you organised a club, you could get an alcohol licence. The sailing club was the preferred haunt after work. There were lots of 16ft Hobie catamarans lined up outside, sun-faded and full of sand, never having touched the water. They were the front for a good piss-up!

We walked into the bar and I saw John Farrell in a corner with Pete Jolly, a health and safety officer whom I knew was also a former Royal Marine. Dixon was at the other side of the bar, so I ordered a pint. About halfway through my pint, I shouted across the bar, "Dixon, I thought I'd introduce you to these two lads as they were also Marines like you." You could have heard a pin drop.

John Farrell opened the dialogue with, "What commando were you in, mate?"

Fair play to Dixon, he came back with, "42, Bickleigh Barracks, Plymouth." He must have done a bit of research, but it took only minutes for his world to crumble,

Pete asked him dates and so on, relevant to 42's movements at that time, and when Dixon falteringly gave them, Pete said, "Then you must have been in Norway at that time, as I was a ski instructor and we had 42 there with us."

"Yeah, that's right."

"What was your location?"

Pause.

"Well, I was shipped home soon after arrival, because I slipped on a wet wooden floor in a bar and broke my leg."

"That wasn't the question, mate. The question was, 'What was your location?'"

Longer pause.

"It was a small village called...Er, near a bigger village called... Ermmmm, phew, I can't remember, it was so long ago."

"No problem, mate."

This went on for ages. They slowly picked him apart. It was like death by a thousand cuts. At one point, Dixon started to look ill, slugged his drink down and headed for the toilets. While he was away, I quickly bought him another pint and placed it in front of his stool so that he had to stay. I stepped back to watch the fun that, by being a total Billy Liar, he had created for himself.

I heard John Farrell pipe up: "What did you specialise in, mate?"

I honestly couldn't believe Dixon's reply. "I was a sniper."

Silence.

Pete Jolly stepped in with, "What weapon did you use, then?"

I almost choked when I heard Dixon's reply. He'd given me a book earlier that he'd finished the day before, about a fictitious rogue US sniper who had used Dixon's weapon of choice. "A Sharp's 30.30."

I leaned back, closed my eyes and filled my lungs with disbelief.

John Farrell broke the silence. "Isn't that what the cowboys shot buffalo with?"

Quick as a flash, Pete served Dixon's coup de grace. "What scope did you use on it?"

There was silence from the end of the bar. Darren Broughton was digging me in the ribs and whispering, "Look at him, look at him." I glanced over, and all I could see were the whites of his eyes. He slowly leaned back and flaked out... Crash! A full faint, straight off his bar stool and on to the wooden floor, much like his fictitious trip to Norway!

An ambulance was called and he was wheeled out of the bar, off to the medical clinic and put under observation for 24 hours. While he was away, the back of his overalls were sprayed with crosshairs. Ruthless, but job done.

A very sheepish, deflated shadow returned to the ship the following evening. I can't remember much about Dixon after this incident, but I heard from others that he has an unbelievably thick skin and was soon up to his old tricks again. Some people never learn.

THE KILLER RIG

In 2000, a jack-up rig, the Al Mariyah, was on location over wellhead tower 94 in the Umm Shaif field in the Persian Gulf. Suddenly, she sent out a mayday call and the barge I was on was instructed to move to its location as soon as possible. Apparently, the Al Mariah had manoeuvred into position and jacked its body just clear of the sea's surface, to standby in that position for a pre-determined time. This allowed the management on board to check that the rig was stable before deploying a derrick out over the adjacent wells.

Later, during cantilever skidding operations, the main deck of the jack-up collapsed, causing the cantilever deck to tilt over. The rig floor fell on to the platform below, damaging the helideck and topside module, while the derrick fell into the sea and sank. The main deck of the jack-up eventually came to rest, floating at sea level. Of 68 workers on board, four Indian and Pakistani men were crushed and died; eight were injured. After the incident, all production wells on the platform were secured, with no oil or gas leaks reported.

When we arrived, the anchor-handling tugs set us up so that our diving baskets were on the rear of the rig to the prevailing swell, and a damage inspection dive was made. The diver's head-mounted camera showed the extent of damage. Its massively reinforced 165-ton legs were completely bent and twisted, and would have to be cut off.

We worked on those legs for a couple of weeks with Broco cutting gear. In the beginning, it was OK, because there was a lot of structural strength present. However, as they were painstakingly cut, they got weaker and weaker. They sounded like a creaking door in a haunted house to us underwater, as the floating rig moved up and down in the swell.

The more we cut, the weaker the legs became. Every dive was like Russian roulette because at some point, it had to go. We cut the underside first and because of the moon phase creating a strong tidal current, we had to tie ourselves to the leg to stay in place. Tied upside down to a 165-ton lump of metal that you were attempting to cut loose was not fun. Even the final cuts on the 12 o'clock position were scary. However, we eventually cut the legs off, recovered them onto our deck, and the rig was towed away. Six years later, after being mothballed, she was refitted and put back to work.

I continued with CCC after this job and ended up on a barge in Egypt. We lived below decks under the massive crane, and as soon as the lights went out, we were invaded by more cockroaches than I had ever seen in one place. This is where my patience finally ran out with the living conditions – the cockroaches were even living in the salad served with the slop every meal-time.

The icing on the cake was a big Sheffield-born diving supervisor, who for reasons known only to him, made a big mistake with depth and time calculations, resulting in me getting decompression sickness or "the bends". It was in my left elbow, but as soon as I was blown back down in the diving chamber on deck, the lodged gas bubble was re-compressed and the pain disappeared. I was slowly brought back to the surface on a therapeutic dive table, but I had seen enough of this cowboy show. For the only time in my life, I quit a diving job and headed to the beach in a tugboat. The supervisor had tried to Tippex the incident out of the log and made a mess of it. These days, that would be enough for a substantial compensation claim.

Once on the beach, a few other guys and I walked along a dusty road and ended up by the side of the main road to Cairo. We were trying to catch a ride but having no luck, until a bus came along and we piled on. The occupants were all a little crazy: there was a man singing and dancing with a skinny white chicken under his arm. Another swaying and constantly muttering under his breath. I made as small an outline as I could and finally made it into a Cairo hotel. This was then followed by the airport, where I checked in as fast as possible and flew home to Sweden.

FINED FOR FIGHTING

After being home for a while, I got an email from an old Swedish diving friend who lived on the outskirts of Stockholm. We arranged to meet a nice old bar called Wirströms.

After a few beers, he asked if I wanted to go to a well-known haunt close by that was open very late. This was only around 21.30 and even though I was happy where I was, I went along. We paid the entrance fee and entered. The place appeared almost empty. My friend had to visit the toilet as he had just broken the three-pint seal, so he left me at the bar and I bought two beers. I had the two glasses in my hands and was walking beside the dance floor when from behind, I was struck between the shoulder blades, and emptied the two glasses onto the floor as I staggered forward.

I turned around in the empty club to see a short, swarthy guy pulling his hands towards himself in the universal language of "Come on". I put the empty glasses on the table, turned around and hit him only once: centre of mass in the middle of his head. I hit him from my ancestors, and knocked him spark out on the floor. The doormen then rocked up. The guy was Turkish and so were they. World War Three ensued.

No matter how tough you think you are, if there are enough opponents, they will win. I ended up face down on the dance floor in the blood and beer, with a pair of handcuffs on. I was then dragged to a back room and sat on some empty beer barrels, with one Turkish doorman pacing up and down. I told him to take the cuffs off and we could sort it out. He stopped directly in front of me and carried out the act of a complete coward, punching me as hard as he could in the face and leaving, locking the door behind him.

Imagine my relief when the door was finally opened and the police came in, to see me bleeding profusely all over my white shirt. I thought I would at least have someone to explain the situation to, but no. They frogmarched me to the police car, drove me a short distance and locked me up.

I sat there all night until around 10.30am, when a completely bored policewoman took a statement and kicked me out. At least you get a breakfast in the UK! I was on the streets in central Stockholm in my white shirt with dried blood and beer stains all over me. People were crossing the street as I approached. I eventually found a taxi rank and as a woman got out, I slipped in. The driver almost had heart failure when he checked his rear-view mirror.

My wife Catrin was obviously highly delighted with my escapades, but my problem was that the night's events had been far from my agenda. It was all started by someone else but here I was, once again the one in trouble.

A few weeks later, I got a letter to say that I was being charged with assault and I had to go to visit a psychiatrist. This was the biggest waste of taxpayers' money I have ever experienced. Every question I answered was recorded and immediately believed with zero confirmation or check on any of them.

"Did your parents drink when you were a child?"

"Nope, not a drop."

"Did your parents smoke?"

"Nope never."

Blah, blah, blah...

I gave her exactly what she wanted to hear during the whole interview and she took everything to be true, which I still find to be a bizarre way of working. I almost told her that where I come from, friends work together on a Friday, fight drunk on a Saturday night and go back to work as friends again on Monday morning. But I was told that in Sweden, that would have been the wrong picture to paint to a pre-trial psychiatrist.

I was assigned a free lawyer who was not at all interested. I went to the hearing with Catrin. A whole school of children seemed to be crammed into the courtroom as part of some project to listen to the day's proceedings. I could see the guy I had hit sitting

102

opposite me, with what looked like a prostitute sitting next to him. She was a scrawny wretch in stiletto heels, micro miniskirt, spray-on Lycra top and make-up by catapult. I had never seen her before.

The female judge kicked the proceedings off with a question directed at her.

"What part do you have to play in the proceedings?"

"I am a witness."

"OK, witnesses will be heard later. So please leave the courtroom and I will call for you when you are required"

I saw her nervously snap a glance at the Turk, whose name I had by now found out was Mr Bullit. I thought directly that they hadn't got their story straight as she click-clacked out of the court room in her ridiculous heels.

I was questioned by the judge and gave a completely true account of the evening's events. The Turk was then questioned and admitted to pushing me from behind. However, he claimed someone pushed him and he was trying to stop himself falling.

"Call the witness."

Click-clack, in she walked. A tall chair was positioned in front of the judge and she perched on top of it with all of her skinny legs on show.

The judge began: "Did you see what happened on the night in question?"

"Yes," (pointing at me). "Him, him, what's he called?"

"Mr Steele."

"Him, he grabbed my man from behind, smashed a glass and pushed it in his face!"

I inwardly laughed and looked across at the scar-free face of her supposed husband.

The judge continued, "Madam, do you realise that if I find you to be lying, I will bring charges against you?"

Silence.

She climbed down off the chair, click-clacked to the sidelines and said nothing more during the proceedings.

The judge then turned to me and said, "Mr Steele, I believe everything you have told me. However, you made Mr Bullit's face bleed. Therefore, under Swedish law, I have no other option than to find you guilty of assault, and I fine you 900 kronor and 2000 kronor for the police fund. This will remain on your record for ten years."

I left the court a free man, but my record was blemished.

I continued with another couple of years' commercial diving in the Persian Gulf and then somehow fell into the next stage of my life. No real planning; it just happened.

Chapter Four

IRAQ

VALHALLA

Warrior, go to your brothers,
Your seat awaits you in Valhalla,
Those who went before wait to fill your cup,
Drink with each, a toast to worthy men.

Dedicated to Neil W,
Swordfish 3 & 5

HEADING FOR A WAR ZONE

During the spring and summer of 2004, I had the notion of working in Sweden and not travelling away any more. A guy I knew owned a landscaping business that involved building a lot of children's playgrounds, so I started working for him. Initially, I was hooked up with a half Jamaican/Swedish guy called Stefan. We worked well together, but my first real indication of the rampant Swedish terror of being branded a racist came when one day during the morning coffee break, I asked Stefan if he was going to work snow-ploughing in the winter. When he said "Yes," I replied, "Good. At least we won't lose you in the snow. We both laughed over this but the other people in the room just stared at me. You could have heard a pin drop!

I got along with most of the people at this time. However, this was the end of working with those whose idea of an adrenaline rush was watching the weekend lottery numbers being drawn. I just couldn't do it anymore, so because Iraq was in the news and ex-military guys I knew from the diving world were heading east, I started seriously researching how to break into private security.

COURSES TO KEEP ME ALIVE

I put my plan into motion in August 2004. Realising I needed some courses and paperwork, I enrolled on a close protection course in Sweden. It was run by a former American Marine.

Freddy, a big guy from Gothenburg and a student on the course, was practising an exfil (extraction) manoeuvre from a restaurant into the back of a Hyundai Santa Fe with a "principal". The principal later apologised for putting his foot on the running board during the manoeuvre, which effectively shoved Freddy into the roof. As mentioned, Freddy was a big strong guy and the principal thought he weighed too much and was afraid of getting hurt. Freddy's head slammed straight into the car's roof edge: he went down on one knee and a fountain of blood poured from his head. He'd ripped a large flap of skin back and literally scalped himself.

With the flap of skin back in place, two field dressings couldn't staunch the flow. A three-hour trip to hospital and a patchwork of stitches gave him a horseshoe scar that will forever remind him (and me) of the event.

This was followed by me heading to hospital, after having three ribs broken in a three-minute session of trying to remain standing while being attacked one by one in quick succession by the other 11 members of the course. One other bloke found out later that he'd also had his ribs broken. The course venue's toilets were decorated with nose blood and toilet roll. We were a sorry-looking bunch by the day's end!

I moved on to a weapons course in Latvia. The guy in charge was a Russian ex-KGB field officer called Boris. He told me that a grey BMW would pick me up outside my hotel at 07.00. To the second, it squealed to a halt outside. We sped off to an underground warehouse/range filled with a thick cloud of Russian cigarette smoke and spent all day doing fire and manoeuvre drills, field-stripping and other drills with an AK74 and 47.

When I had successfully completed the course, Boris told me to spread the word among my friends that he could arrange anything from flying a MiG to driving a tank, or anything in between!!!

I then did a one-on-one course on the Glock family with the Latvian practical pistol champion. The sport of practical pistol shooting is based on combat pistol techniques and takes the form of simulations of defensive or combat situations. It was a good course but I never liked the Glock. There's a safety-catch issue (for me, it just hasn't got one, no matter what the manufacturer says) and it also feels like a plastic toy. No matter how many rounds I put down, I just couldn't get tight consistent grouping, unlike the heavier metal CZ75 Para or Browning hi-power, with which, if you ran out of rounds, you could at least club someone to death!

A TERRIFYING "TACTICAL LANDING"

In early October, I got an interview in London with a private security company operating in Iraq that was looking for operators. I turned up 15 minutes early at an impressive building and was taken to the CEO's office. The interview was conducted by an ex-Gurkha officer who I will call NB. I had been working off and on in the Middle East since 1982, and was well versed with the Arabic ways, so he liked that. In the middle of the interview, however, he suddenly flew off on a different tangent, leapt halfway over the table with a sudden: "Have you ever been under fire?" I came back with an affirmative, because when I had worked for Algosaibi in northern Saudi, my ship had been shelled when the first Gulf War kicked off. It was large-calibre but I had definitely been under fire!

The interview ended abruptly. We went to the upper floor and carried out a lot of admin. During this, I filled in one ominous document that had a section with a bold red heading. Basically, it said that if you had been charged with any *serious* offence, you had to fill it in. I pondered over this because my assault charge was in another country. However, I decided to come clean and explained my story to NB. He said, "Did you go to prison?"

"Nope."

"F**k it, then. Leave it blank."

I was asked to visit a doctor's practice for a DNA test, in case I ended up crispy, and was informed that I would deploy to Baghdad the following Friday.

I quit my Swedish job which involved building kids' playgrounds, packed my kit and said goodbye to my wife and two-year-old twins. Catrin was happy for me, as staying at home permanently, for me, was like caging an animal. I had worked away from home my whole life and needed some excitement.

Before I knew it, I was back at Heathrow waiting to fly to Baghdad via Amman in Jordan. I had been told to hook up in Heathrow with two others, Mick Cahill and Chris Mitchel. We bounced through Amman and were on (strangely enough) an old Swedish aircraft heading for Baghdad. We droned along for a while and were fed the standard dry piece of cake that was always served by the South African crew, when suddenly, everything tilted sharply to the left. The engines screamed as if they were being ripped from the wings and we plummeted downwards in a 45-degree spiral! I looked at some of the other passengers and couldn't see much alarm from any of them. I tightened my seatbelt as much as I could and hung on. Suddenly the plane levelled, flared and hit the ground with a thump. Welcome to Iraq!

I didn't know that this was a tactical landing used by all commercial and cargo flights. From cruising height, the plane would spiral down within the huge perimeter of the airport to avoid small arms fire, rocket-propelled grenades (RPGs) and ground-to-air missiles. I wish someone had told us before it happened. On future trips, I would look forward to this. The reverse procedure was applied on return trips to Jordan: a quick take-off followed by a tight spiral climb to cruising altitude and then heading west.

$5 MILLION, HIDDEN UNDER A BED

Induction training took place in a big warehouse next to Saddam's Presidential Palace and pool. On completion, I was told I would be heading to Mosul to join a team in Forward Operating Base (FOB) Freedom. We did the Route Irish run through Checkpoint 12 back to Baghdad airport and were kicking our heels waiting for the US military flight to Mosul, when an American guy walked up and said, "Excuse me, guys. Can you take this with you? It will be collected at the other end." I can't remember who actually took the plastic bag, but he disappeared as fast as he'd arrived. When we looked inside, it was stacked with bundles of US currency.

We boarded the C130 and landed in Mosul, expecting someone to pounce on us for the cash, but nothing. It was too late for the team from FOB Freedom to cross town and pick us up, so we were given a bed for the night. Of course, the plastic bag was emptied and pictures taken: $525,000 in what looked like a plastic supermarket bag, given to four strangers. How weird is that? Early the next morning, there was a knock and a guy said, "I believe you have something for me." The bag was handed over. It was cash for the reconstruction, which I will explain later.

We had arrived at the height of the 2004 battle of Mosul, the capital of the Ninewa Governorate. This occurred concurrent to heavy fighting in Fallujah. Over the next three weeks, 76 bodies of executed Iraqi soldiers were found throughout the city and 122 people were killed during street fighting: four US soldiers, 31 members of the Iraqi security forces, nine Kurdish Peshmerga fighters, at least 71 insurgents, five civilians, one British security contractor doing the same job as me and a Turkish truck driver. With that, the final death toll of the insurgent uprising in Mosul was an estimated 198 killed.

However, other estimates are much higher and some sources say many more insurgents and civilians were killed in the battle. Actual casualty figures remain unknown. The insurgents managed to make a haven out of the western part of the city, from where they continued to conduct hit-and-run attacks over the coming months – and through which we regularly travelled to and from the Syrian border.

The team from FOB Freedom collected us and we bundled into armoured Toyota Land Cruisers and headed across town. Fifteen minutes later, we were given our beds. Over the next few months, we were constantly mortared and rocketed. Our medic had already been badly wounded by a falling mortar round and shipped out.

My first trip was north into Kurdistan, to the Turkish border town of Harbur Gate. We would crew-change in and out of the country through this route, drop off in Harbur Gate and head over the border. In Turkey, we would experience an extremely dodgy four-hour taxi ride past a place called Batman, then on to Diyabikir, before flying to Istanbul and home. Even lying unarmed and alone in a hotel bed in what was supposed to be the safety of Diyabikir, I would hear gunshots. It was definitely not a place for an evening stroll. Waiting on the Iraqi side for people coming off leave and over the border, we would be surrounded by street urchins, all professing to be starving. We would cook up a few MREs, which stands for "meals ready to eat", but we translated them as "meals rejected by Ethiopians". Often it was pork and beans, but even though they were Muslim, the urchins never complained.

I had joined the team while they were doing many missions in Kurdistan, ferrying a Filipino/US Navy woman I'll call Rosie around with rucksacks full of dollars to pay for reconstruction work. The cash we had been given in Baghdad was involved in this process. On one of these trips, while I was driving Rosie in the Bravo vehicle along with the cash, we were on the wrong end of a small arms attack from rooftops on the outskirts of Mosul. After returning to the FOB and looking the vehicles over, we found that they had missed with every round!

The official company report went as follows...

AMBUSH ON PSD IN MOSUL – 27 NOV – UPDATED
Posted: 27 November 2004 09:23 (GST)
1045 hrs 27th November 2004 XXXX Contact Report

Whilst travelling south along a main road in Mosul in the area of grid 38SLF380216, a 3 vehicle XXXX convoy noticed it was being followed by a Dark Blue BMW with front fog lights. It was not possible to see any occupants.
As the XXXX team carried out a planned U turn they also saw an Orange and White taxi (on video) parked in the centre of the road. The BMW then flashed its fog lights and stopped by the taxi. The driver's side taxi door was then opened. Having negotiated the U turn, the team came under small arms fire from multiple locations, including the area of the Taxi/BMW which was now to their rear.

Comment. It is thought the occupants of the BMW left that car and also fired at the team.
The team then saw a Blue/White Small bus block one side of the road and the two occupants run from it.

Comment. The team believe this to have been a deliberate attempt to force them down a side street adjacent to the Bus. This is supported by team member observations of a group of four males on a rooftop along that road. And that the road was partially blocked by a group of cars.

The team avoided the bus and drove through the ambush area coming under sustained fire from both sides of the road including automatic fire with tracer. Over 100 rounds were fired at the team. As they left the ambush area, they observed the same BMW following them at a distance. The BMW was subsequently lost due to aggressive driving by the team.
No fire was returned, there were no casualties and there were no hits on the XXXX callsigns.

Summary.
This was a complex attack involving a surveillance car, multiple firing points and a possible attempt to force the team along a specific route. Team members believe that had they taken that forced route, they would have come under SAF and IED attack.

The team successfully carried out their SOPs and drove through the ambush.

This route is rarely used by XXXX and therefore it is thought that this was an attack planned for any suitable target passing through that area and not specific to this XXXX callsign.

One client was travelling with the team. This person was not injured.

We resupplied, then moved out the same day, using a different route to Sulaymaniyah. This time, we arrived at or destination without incident and Rosie was given a room in a big, secure hotel in the centre of town. Her room was sandwiched between ours and she was given a radio and spare battery with strict instructions to call us whenever she needed anything. The team then split into two shifts and the first went to the restaurant to eat. As soon as we ordered our food, Rosie walked in: no radio call; nothing! "Rosie, where is the money?" asked the team leader.

"Don't worry, boys," she said. "I hid it under the bed." We are talking about two large red rucksacks containing a total of (as I was later told) $5 million!

The way it worked for these reconstruction projects was like this. We would take Project and Completing Office (PCO) personnel or in Baghdad, the Corp of Engineers, to a location after studying surroundings and associated mapping/intelligence reports. A 20-minute on-site cut-off time was normally given to complete any inspection work. Planning would then be formulated by American engineers for the rebuild of the building or structure and tenders would be submitted. When a local company was selected as the winner, a pre-determined amount of money would be released to them, so they could begin work. When the project reached a certain level of build, engineers would visit the site unannounced, escorted by one of our teams. We would leave 20 minutes later by an alternative route. If the build was to a satisfactory standard and stage of completion, we would again escort the money person to a safe meeting point and deliver the cash for the next stage of the project. This would continue, in theory, until the reconstruction project was completed. That said, in all my time

114

in Iraq, I can never recall escorting anyone to view the successful completion of any project.

THE SUICIDE BOMBER

During one extended time away from our FOB, we stayed over in the compound in Irbil and were prepping for a long day's driving around Kurdistan. All three vehicles pulled out of the compound to find fuel. We had a cash fund of dollars for emergencies, and as there was no regular fuel supply, it was covered by the cash.

We found a likely bunch of kids at the side of the road with various fuel drums, so I slid into position and jumped out, smelled the fuel to confirm that it was petrol and indicated to the kid to fill both long-range tanks. The team were out on foot, giving me 360° cover as the petrol poured into my V8 Land Cruiser. Once I was done, I performed a U-turn to allow the second (diesel) vehicle into position. I saw the vehicle commander leap out and start pointing at the car's rear and shouting at the kids. They were obviously trying to tell him something, but he was getting more and more irritated, so the leader of the kids eventually shrugged and poured the fuel in. The next scene was like slow motion. The vehicle commander leaned forward to screw on the fuel cap, took a closer look, sniffed the fuel that had spilled on the side of the vehicle, then to my horror, for reasons known only to him, pulled out a lighter and lit it. A flame shot down the side of the Land Cruiser and onto the puddle on the ground. The driver saw the flash in his mirror, started the motor and quickly drove out of the fire. The kids helped put out the fire on his tyre with handfuls of sand – but the car had been filled with paraffin! The kids had tried to tell him. However, with his aggressive behaviour they had given in and just filled it up.

We returned to the compound to pick up the clients immediately, so for the rest of the day, I followed a vehicle that stank like an old paraffin lamp. It was very sluggish but it managed to run all day! We eventually diluted the paraffin with another resupply of diesel and when we made it back to our

116

home base in Mosul, the mechanics were surprised and highly impressed that the big Toyota's diesel motor had kept going.

Just after the fuel incident, three clients were dropped off in FOB Marez, the Mosul airbase. After a run across town from FOB Freedom, my team was driving past the American DEFAC, the big military mess hall. The team leader stopped his Alpha vehicle and asked over the radio if the team wanted to eat there or back in FOB Freedom. General agreement was to push on, as it was always a hassle to get out of body armour and so on. The three-vehicle convoy exited the airbase and dashed across town. As soon as the vehicles arrived in FOB Freedom, the airwaves were full of frantic chatter. Just a few minutes after the team had passed the DEFAC, a 24-year-old Mosul resident, who had been working in the base for two months, had donned an explosives vest under an Iraqi uniform and walked into the DEFAC. He made straight for a large group of soldiers and detonated himself. A total of 72 people were injured and 22 killed in the blast, with 14 of the dead being US soldiers. Ansar al-Sunna claimed responsibility for the attack. Our team had been very, very, lucky.

As the end of 2004 was looming, a little New Year party was becoming more than probable. I bought a litre bottle of Absolut Mandrin Vodka in Kurdish Sulaymaniyah, costing just $3. It had been transported all the way from Sweden, yet the guy was still obviously making a profit!

After buying the New Year booze stock, the team jumped into the wagons and headed to a well-known burger eatery in town called MaDonels. Yup, you read it right. Somehow, the translation had got messed up but these home-made burgers beat McDonald's hands down. It was really good food, though I am still not sure what kind of meat it was.

IRANIAN BORDER SMUGGLERS

A couple of months later, after charging all over north-western Iraq, my luck run out. Our boss was volunteering us for some strange and extremely dodgy tasks. The American military wouldn't do a job on the Iranian border because it was too far away for any effective ground support, but the boss immediately said, "My lads will do it." So off we went (minus him, of course) to check out a border post and video the whole route – it was basically a free route reconnaissance and cross-border surveillance mission of smuggling activity for the American military.

The trip involved no dramas but close to Halabja, I saw two kids in separate locations were running on all fours like dogs, and one had a really long tongue flapping around lower than his chin. I still wonder if this was something to do with Saddam's gassing of the population in that area a few years previously.

This trip took us through beautiful scenery with lots of high-walled passes. As we crested the tops of mountains, we could see snow-topped mountain ranges for miles. We were warned by the Peshmerga (the Kurdish military), not to stray off-road because the area was strewn with land mines. In places, the mines could be seen lying at the side of the road as they were constantly being washed down hillsides to rest on the first flat ground they settled on – the road.

As we closed on the border with Iran, the road turned to mud. We noticed makeshift shelters in a lot of the small wadis bordering the route, so we stopped and our Peshmerga translator spoke to the occupants. It transpired that the tarpaulin shelters held case upon case of canned German beer destined to end up over the border. No-one likes to do an empty return trip over the border, but when the smugglers were asked what cargo they carried on the return journey, the atmosphere went frosty. I can only surmise that the return cargo began its life growing as a little red flower in an Afghan field.

On arrival at the physical border with Iran, we got out of the vehicles for a leg stretch. We were above the snow line and I looked out over a massive valley. In the distance, on the side of the next mountain, I could see a long pack mule/horse train bypassing the border and heading into Iran. I grabbed my video camera and filmed it all.

After we had observed the to and fro movement through the border and collected enough video footage, we headed back. As we broke through the snow line, it started to rain. JB, sitting next to me, started shouting through fits of laughter: "Look at that! Look at that!" A guy was driving towards us in a car that defied the laws of science. It looked like it had been chewed on by a herd of dinosaurs. He had no windscreen, lights or paint. Mud and rain were pouring into the vehicle but what had caught JB's attention was the fact that the driver of this contraption, covered in mud, was lying forward on the steering wheel and leaning out of the hole where the windscreen had once been, with a pair of bright pink diving goggles on!

Kurdish/Iranian smugglers with pack horses resting in a wadi

PISTOLS IN ISTANBUL

As stated earlier, the route out of the country at this time was across the Iraqi/Kurdish border, then through Diyabakir to Istanbul and home. I had an incident in Istanbul on one of these trips, which was entirely of my own making. I was walking along a well-used tourist street in the middle of town, just window shopping and doing a bit of sightseeing, while I killed time before my flight home the following evening. A guy stopped and asked in very good English if I was an English tourist, I said no, that I was an oilfield worker and was making my way home from Abu Dhabi. He talked for a while and told me that he had been a horse veterinarian for an Arab family in Abu Dhabi and talked about different venues around the town. Luckily, I was fully aware of the places he was talking about and he asked if I fancied a quick beer in a good bar he knew. I agreed and followed him into a busy bar that held a lot of local office workers taking a drink before heading home. He bought the first round and it went on like that for a few hours. The guy was really funny and good company. The bar was emptying, so he asked if I would join him at another venue... Why not? I was just killing time, after all.

After a quick taxi ride that I paid for, as he had jumped in the back (that should have been an indicator), we pulled up at a club. He jumped out, I paid the driver and we entered. The staff were all over him and treated him like royalty. A waiter showed us to a table and instantly carrot and cucumber sticks in a glass container complete with dip arrived. A second waiter arrived and asked what I wanted to drink. As I was sick of beer by now, I asked for a vodka and coke. My new "friend" took the same and as I took a sip, three female east European "employees" of the club sat down at the table. This is when I started to look for an exit from the situation...

The guy was cracking jokes and ordering more vodka. He asked if we could split the bill at the end, which I agreed to, but as my third drink arrived, he said he was going to the toilet. He left and a couple of minutes later, the girl who had been sitting next to him left too. I sat and sipped my drink and waited for his return so that I could thank him and leave. About 20 minutes passed, so I decided to go. I squeezed past the two bored east European women remaining, and made for the door. This is where my problems began.

I explained that I had been with their friend and as he had disappeared, I had to leave. I said I would pay half of the drinks, so what do I owe? After a frantic pushing of buttons on a large calculator, a figure flashed up in red on a cash counter... HOW MUCH?!! I got my phone out and did a calculation. It was just over £800 for five vodkas and coke, a few cucumber and carrot slices – oh, and some unintelligible nonsense from his east European friends.

I told the cashier that I couldn't pay that much but he could check on my card to see how much I could pay. He took it and eventually removed the £25 I knew was in that account. I told him I could go to my hotel and return with the balance but what happened next, I really didn't see coming. He told me in a menacing voice that one of his men would accompany me to my hotel and I would find a way to pay or... At the word "or", he pulled the front of his man's suit to expose a pistol in a shoulder holster. This guy was the size of a house.

They brought a car to the door and me and the giant climbed in the back. My mind was racing as he asked for the name of my hotel. I lied and blurted out "The Hilton." Off we sped through dingy Turkish back streets.

As we pulled up to the Hilton, I had formulated my plan. I told the giant that as I was an oilfield worker, I had a lot of cash with me and I would be right back. Amazingly, he just stood by the car as I entered the hotel. I walked straight up to the reception desk and asked a young guy if there was an alternative exit from the hotel. He pointed to the bar, so I took off, straight through the bar and out into an alleyway. I knew the direction of my hotel, as I had walked past the Hilton earlier in the day, so I just kept the waterfront on my right side and arrived at the Queen Seagull Hotel around 30 minutes later.

I gave the receptionist a brief rundown of my problem, and he said "Don't worry, things like this happen all the time in Istanbul. I will say you checked out if someone comes." Once in my room, I had time to think, so I packed my bag and headed back downstairs to check out properly. I then waited in a darkened alley opposite the hotel until a taxi arrived with guests. Once they exited the taxi, I jumped in and was transported to the airport. I lived in the airport for almost 24hrs but it was a lot better than meeting the giant and his pistol again.

THE MINE THAT ALMOST GOT US

Following my leave and back in the relative safety of FOB Freedom, we were told by the boss to resupply immediately, get some sleep and head to the Syrian border the following morning with an American long-range reconnaissance patrol (LRRP) to check on border posts.

This guy, who constantly sent us far and wide into some of the most dangerous places on the planet, wouldn't even run with us across Mosul. When it was time for him to go on leave, he would insist on a ride in an armoured American Stryker. Never once did he attempt the dodgy run over the Iraqi border and out through Turkey like the rest of us: it was a fixed-wing from Mosul airbase for him every time. Whatever happened to "leading from the front"?

On the way out of Mosul, embedded with the LRRP patrol at around 3am the following morning, I was following a Humvee. As we went around the infamous Yarmuk turning circle, which is basically a big open roundabout, I looked left and saw a large golden-coloured cooking oil can on a breeze block, with scarlet detonating cord running down the side of it. IED! The call went out, but we had all passed it without any bang. We pulled over next to a high wall and the Americans called it in. My vehicle commander got out and we had a tense 40 minutes in the suburban darkness with lights flashing on and off in alleyways, until an American explosive ordnance disposal team arrived and dealt with it. Lucky call – the trigger man must have gone for a cuppa as we passed.

We continued the mission with no further incident. But as we entered the infamous town of Tal Afar in the dark, I saw the Alpha vehicle ahead swerve to the right. Before I could react, I saw the dreaded array of short prongs sticking out of the road. Insurgents would lay a landmine in a pothole, then fill around it with a mix of sand and oil to resemble the asphalt road surface.

124

The prongs went under the vehicle and I drove over them, the mine passed straight down the centre of my vehicle.

The vehicle comms kit with the PANIC box on the right

Around two or three or seconds later, there was an almighty blast and the rear of my vehicle was briefly lifted off the ground. The mine had gone off between my vehicle and the Humvee behind! Lucky or what? We sustained no serious damage and no injuries. I spoke to an American EOD specialist about this a couple of weeks later, and he thought that it was may have been rigged to a hidden command wire that had been initiated at the wrong time, or possibly the first Land Cruiser had clipped a prong on the mine. It was known that some of the Russian anti-tank mines being used by insurgents had a defective fuse, on occasion.

This was just prior to the battle of Al Quaim, or Operation Matador. We were charging along the Syrian border, gathering as much human intelligence (HUMINT) as possible from border posts, then lying up at night in the Sinjar Mountains. I found out much later that during one of his many border post-interviews, the client/translator we had with us had located the whereabouts of one of Saddam Hussein's very close relatives.

This was passed down the chain of command and he was the recipient of a night-time helicopter-borne snatch team.

HIT WITH AN RPG

While working on the border, a silver Japanese pickup tried to do a quick detour around a snap vehicle checkpoint (VCP) that we had set up. The Americans immediately charged off across the desert in their Humvees in pursuit. The occupants were all arrested and interrogated. It turned out they had stolen uniforms, body armour weapons and the vehicle. They were duly handed over to the Iraqi border guards, and we thought that their nightmare of captivity had just begun. However, as we were heading towards the next border post, we saw them driving off in the opposite direction over the desert behind us – in their stolen pickup. The border guards had released them as soon as we left.

By February 22, 2005, we had gathered all the intelligence we needed. We were returning to Mosul and passed through a dusty and ominously deserted village called Tall Uwaynat. Beyond the village, the road was straight but it dipped for a couple of kilometres, with a collapsed blue-and-white police building on the right side, in the bottom of the dip. From this building, a road ran to the right at 90 degrees directly to Tal Afar – the scene of the earlier mine incident and a hotbed of insurgent activity. This junction was lined with fruit and veg stands with tall sand berms that could afford concealment to a few cars and more importantly, enemy fighters.

I was driving the Bravo vehicle with a Kurdish client sitting directly behind me. As we approached the collapsed building, a figure in black robes ran into the middle of the road, dropped to one knee and threw an RPG launcher onto his shoulder. He snapped off a shot that cleared the Alpha vehicle in front of me then missed my roof by about a metre. Alpha peeled off left to do a U-turn and I peeled off right. Charlie vehicle went nose-up to a small brick building on the right side of the road, effectively shielded from incoming small arms and RPG fire, which was intense within seconds.

I can never look at Hollywood war films in the same light after my Iraqi experiences. That RPG incident is still fresh in my memory. When someone launches one at you, there is no

JB, LRRPs and the enemy

dive to the left, dive to the right or duck. It is *instantly* on you at over 300 metres per second. It either hits or misses.

As I U-turned, my left side wheels slipped off the tarmac into the gooey mud and the vehicle hesitated. I slipped into four-wheel drive and gassed it. My vehicle took the brunt of incoming belt-fed PKM light machine gun and AK47 fire from insurgents hidden in the fruit and veg stands and those sand berms. The rounds hitting the vehicle's armour sounded like sledgehammers and eventually, at least one found a weak spot and entered the engine bay. I could feel the engine dying as I desperately tried to move away from the junction. A few seconds later, I ended up facing away from the contact point with a dead engine stuck in first gear, holding the key down and chugging up the road with flat tyres and moving on the batteries and starter motor! We came to a grinding halt in the middle of the kill zone, the world erupting around us.

Suddenly, I caught movement and a flash out of my peripheral vision to the left. Bang! Bang! I took a huge, almost simultaneous double impact somewhere in the rear of the vehicle. All loose gear in the back was thrown around as if caught in an internal whirlwind.

A chemical light-stick came flying in what seemed to be slow motion through the gap between me and the guy in the passenger seat. It hit the windscreen and landed on the dashboard. It was out of its plastic wrapper and glowing bright green from the impact.

Multiple RPGs were being fired at us but luckily they were missing and impacting in the boggy ground beyond the vehicle with a bang and a plume of brown earth.

My client, a battle-worn Peshmerga man who was also our translator, had a personal protection officer (PPO) assigned to him, who was in the front passenger seat when the incident kicked off. He was South African, claimed to have been a colonel and thought very highly of himself. However, when the vehicle stopped, he managed to turn himself around on his seat with his bulky body armour and mag carrier on, looked out of the back window and screamed as loud as a man can scream: "The RPG's reloading," at which point he hopped out of the vehicle and gave it Billy big-steps up the road, leaving the client (and me) behind.

The RPG guy snapped off another shot but this time it was directed towards the Charlie vehicle, which was still taking cover behind the small concrete building. It exploded harmlessly on a wall, so I took my chance to get out of my crippled vehicle. I dropped the passenger seat back, reached in and dragged the client clear, then took cover in front of the engine block. The smell of hot oil filled the air as the last of the engine's lifeblood drained out onto the highway.

I got through five magazines, returning fire at the numerous tell-tale dust clouds from enemy muzzle blasts on a berm. Although I had already been shot at, this was the first time I had heard

129

rounds actually snapping around me. They were close – very close. The driver and vehicle commander of the Charlie vehicle (Aidy and Richard) reversed away from the bullet and RPG-scarred brick building they had initially sheltered behind and used my vehicle as cover from the incoming fire to crossdeck us. Aidy would tell me later never to shave off my slowly whitening beard, as he thought I was dead until he saw my head moving on the other side of the heavily tinted vehicle windows.

Once aboard, we backed away from my stricken vehicle and formed up with the Eagle team that had been travelling the same route, a one-kilometre tactical distance behind us.

On the in-car video that was recording everything, you can hear me say, "They RPGd me," and "My car is blown to f***ing bits."

We got through a total of 3400 rounds in the ensuing firefight. All vehicles took rounds in the contact, with burst tyres and shot-off wing mirrors and so on, but amazingly, no one was injured.

The South African PPO's weapon was still cold at the end of the contact. He fired exactly zero rounds and contributed nothing to the day's events. After the gunfire was over, he lay on the road and briefly tried to gather sympathy with a fake "bad back" injury from the RPG impact. The military report was "a blow to the head on the windscreen" but was incorrect. Everyone ignored him, so he quickly forgot about that ploy and stood up again. So if you ever read this, DK: as the designated PPO, you were a coward on the day. The whole team knew it. You abandoned your client and ran away.

The hole from a 40mm projectile that went straight through both sides of my armoured vehicle, passing between me and my client without exploding

An F18 appeared, booming overhead 20 minutes after the initial contact, and a couple of Apache attack helicopters were over us 15 minutes later, doing what they do best.

Before we left the location, the fixed-wing aircraft had asked (via our ops room) for permission to take out my incapacitated vehicle. We declined the offer, as mistakes had been made in the past and all of our vehicles looked alike. Fair enough: mine was on fire and smoking heavily, but you never know with any air assets!

My vehicle had been hit too hard to recover. The engine block had been struck by multiple rounds and all of the oil had been dumped. An anti-personnel RPG round had impacted just under the petrol filler cap (thanks to whoever designed explo-safe for fuel tanks) and blew the internal rear armoured door off its hinges from the inside out. A second projectile of around 40mm had entered the vertical door jamb between me and the translator on the seat behind me. It skimmed over his

One of the two Apaches sent to assist

knees, breaking the back of my seat, then exited straight through the right side of the vehicle without going bang. All I had was a nick in my body armour back plate from some flying debris, which I hadn't even noticed in the melee.

Once we had transferred all the kit that had been salvaged from my wagon and changed bullet-riddled wheels on the other vehicles, the team leader dropped a thermite grenade into my vehicle through the driver's side door, as it was not fit for recovery and couldn't be left for the insurgents to salvage.

The Toyota was soon ablaze and the Apaches escorted us home to FOB Freedom. Flying out to our sides at 90 degrees like a pair of giant, deadly dragonflies, they were a very welcoming sight.

My distant downed wagon abandoned in the kill zone top left.
Cross decking under heavy enemy fire, bottom right.

AT 1350C, XXXXX ALERTED TFF THAT THEIR BORDER ASSESSMENT
TEAM RETURNING TO MOSUL TOOK RPG AND SAF AT KF67786178.
ONE VEHICLE WAS DISABLED AND ONE MINOR INJURY DUE TO
HARD VEHICLE MANOEUVRE, HIT HEAD ON WINDSHIELD. AIF BROKE
CONTACT WHEN HEARD FIX WING ARRIVE ON STATION. AEGIS WILL
BLOW VEHICLE IN PLACE AND CONTINUE BACK TO MOSUL. NO CF
INJ/DAMAGE, 1X CIV INJ (MINOR) 1X CIV TRUCK DAMAGED
(CATASTROPHIC).
Report key: 9439E74D-DD41-45C4-9613-54A4B43B39E1
Tracking number: NB-N-47452728
Attack on: ENEMY
Complex attack: FALSE
Reporting unit: Not Provided
Unit name: Not provided
Type of unit: None Selected
Originator group: UNKNOWN
Updated by group: UNKNOWN
MGRS: 38S KF67786178
CCIR:
Sigact:
DColor: RED

Posted: 22 February 2005 15:16 (GST)
On the 22 Feb 05 at 1341hrs a PSD team on Route NAPLES, 70 km North West of Mosul, was ambushed by 20 AIF and attacked by three RPG's and SAF. The commanders of both vehicles were able to hit their transponder panic buttons. So while the team was dismounting and winning the firefight, the alarm was being raised in the RROC in Mosul and the ROC in Baghdad. The military were quickly alerted, thus enabling them to get fixed wing assets over the PSD team within 20 minutes. A rotary QRF was put on standby and was used to escort the team safely to their home base in Mosul.

Back in the FOB, we were met by the boss who asked for volunteers for an ammo run to Tikrit the following day. I was still full of adrenaline and buzzing from the contact a few hours earlier, so I said, "I'll go." A shortlist of seven men was drawn up for the three vehicles. DK didn't offer his services (not that I would have accepted him in the vehicle). I had a former Royal Marine called Darrel Johnson to travel with me as vehicle commander. This I was happy with, so I grabbed some food, went to my room and got my head down.

AMBUSH, AND ENEMY FIRE
EVERYWHERE

Next day, I was issued the keys to my new $200,000 armoured Land Cruiser. As we left Mosul, I mentioned on the radio that it felt more sluggish than the old one but we pressed on, passing through Kirkuk and arriving on Route Clemson, the final main road that would take us over the old riveted steel bridge into Saddam's home town of Tikrit.

We were in the middle of nowhere and labouring up a long straight incline, when we noticed a black BMW saloon parked on our side of the road, facing in our direction of travel. It was called in over the radio and all three vehicles confirmed that they had "eyes on".

As we closed on the BMW, it did a quick U-turn back towards us and drove past our convoy. I can clearly remember the driver's face: he sported a small pointed beard, and had hate oozing out of his eyes. There were four men in the car and they weren't your typical skinny Iraqis.

The BMW disappeared from my view as we crested the hill, but Charlie vehicle called in that it had U-turned and had been joined by a couple of Toyota pickups from a wadi, with a large amount of men aboard each.

As I checked my mirrors, I saw the BMW closing on the Charlie vehicle. Its roof suddenly seemed to be lifted off and blew away. Two men stood up in the car. One opened up with a 7.62mm PKM belt-fed machine-gun and the other started popping RPG rounds at us. They were impacting all around us, and my vehicle was hit by small arms fire, followed by a strong sulphur smell. Darrell, in the passenger seat of my Land Cruiser, lost HF comms with our base in Mosul and we came under heavy fire from wadis on both sides of the road, as we sped up and tried to break contact. We found out later that a PKM tracer round had entered my left rear light, skimmed down the rear wing between

135

the armour and soft skin, cutting the HF radio antenna in the process. It impacted the door armour, broke a weld and entered the vehicle. The same round crossed the back seat, ripping it open until it hit the inside of the right rear door and stopped. If anyone had been sitting on the back seat, the round would have cut through both legs.

This was in the early days and our vehicles hadn't yet been fitted with any rear-fighting capability. Mick Gill was hanging out of the rear door of the Charlie vehicle, another guy hanging onto his belt while he returned fire with a belt-fed Minimi machine-gun.

We knew that there was a major police checkpoint a few kilometres ahead that straddled the road, so we were desperately trying to make it there for backup. As we closed on the police station, there was a textbook "dead dog IED" in the middle of the road, covered with stones. Alpha and Bravo vehicles swerved and passed it but Charlie vehicle got it. Boom! This was almost immediately followed by an extremely near-miss RPG impact at the rear of their vehicle – the same one Aidy and Richie had saved me with the day before.

We barrelled into the checkpoint, expecting to see friendly forces preparing to engage the enemy at our rear. But all I could see were black-clad insurgents running around within the checkpoint, opening up with AKs. I have often found during my life that, even in dire circumstances, there is always room for a little humour. Mo Hurley was Jim B's driver, and as they approached the checkpoint, Jim was looking anxiously back towards my Bravo and the Charlie wagon at the rear, with a procession of insurgents' vehicles chasing us.

He called out to Mo, "Stop inside the checkpoint!"

Mo snapped back, "F**k that, they've taken it!"

"What?"

Mo came back, "It looks like the start of the London Marathon in there!"

We flew through the chicanes in the checkpoint under fire, and took cover behind some HESCO barriers (large bags of sand) before debussing (exiting the vehicles) and engaging the enemy. This was followed by the most intense firefight I experienced in Iraq, where we traded fire with the enemy, who were only approximately 50 to 75m from us.

During the firefight, two of our guys, Jim B and Richie, both had stoppages with their short-barrelled Bushmaster M4s. Richie went down on one knee behind the barrier to clear his weapon and a split-second later, an RPG round clipped the top of the barrier where he'd been standing a moment before. The 40mm projectile tumbled and clattered, hissing down the tarmac, and stopped directly in front of my vehicle. I remember a moment when one of the insurgents scrambled over a sand berm to my left and was shot. He toppled over backwards, his arms held out wide, with a black beard and white flowing robes.

At this point in the firefight, we were being engaged from a small tubular concrete tower within the compound. I could see muzzle flashes coming from the darkness of a small window, so I put what was left of my magazine through it and we received no more fire from that position. Aidy was banging away with his AK next to my right ear and through the madness of battle, for some reason, I gave him a bollocking because of the noise!

An RPG-wielding insurgent stepped out from the HESCO barriers, dropped to one knee, and Aidy got to him before me. Two arms snaked out from behind the HESCOs, grabbed his ankles and dragged him out of sight.

Darrell, a former Royal Marine who was my vehicle commander on the day, was hosing down the enemy vehicles, in case they followed us once we broke contact. But by this time, they were getting organised and beginning to flank us. Jim B, the team leader, ordered us back into the vehicles to make a dash down the arrow-straight road leading away from the checkpoint towards Tikrit. Charlie vehicle could be driven no further because of the earlier battle damage, so Richie shouted that he wanted a thermite grenade to burn it out. Mine had been used on my wagon the day before, so all I could do was pass him a green smoke grenade, in the hope that it would set the seats on fire. As I held it out to him, a couple of tracer rounds passed between us. He gave up on the "torch the vehicle" idea and scrambled into the back of my wagon with the other two guys, as dust erupted around us from the ever-increasing incoming fire.

Even though I had told everyone earlier that the new car was sluggish, it flew down the road as I drove away from the kill zone, my foot hard to the floor. My vehicle was a shambles, with gear and passengers everywhere. I kept inadvertently touching red-hot weapon barrels as I changed gear. We had all collected a few blisters by the time we arrived at our company's base in Tikrit. Somehow, I had collected a bit of Minimi link (the metal belt that holds the bullets together) in my lip. But this was nothing compared with what could – and in all reality, should have happened. We were on the receiving end of 17 RPG rounds. It was a mini-miracle that we all walked out relatively unscathed.

The most important lesson I learned from these back-to-back contacts were that once you are stuck into a firefight, you invariably experience tunnel vision. Nothing is more important to you than the target you are attempting to drop. So no matter what is happening, always watch your flank.

The downed Charlie vehicle was later recovered in one piece by the American quick-reaction force (QRF). Nothing had been touched. It was explained to us that this insurgent cell was absolutely rigid on its cut-off times. They knew how long it took the quick reaction force to respond, so if they hadn't won a battle after a set time, they would just fade into the desert villages and regroup for another attempt.

AT 1250C, AN XXXXX PSD TEAM FROM FOB FREEDOM WAS ATTACKED ON ROUTE CLEMSON BY ROUGHLY 20-30 AIF. THREE VEHICLES (1 BLACK BMW and 2 WHITE PICKUP TRUCKS) CAME UP BEHIND THE PSD TEAM AND PUSHED THEM INTO A KILL ZONE WHERE 20-30 AIF ENGAGED THEM ON THE SIDE OF THE ROAD WITH RPGS AND SMALL ARMS FIRE. THE ATTACK AGAINST THE PSD TEAM LEFT ONE TOYOTA LAND CRUISER DISABLED. NO PERSONNEL WOUNDED. THE 116 BCT DISPATCHED TWO PLATOONS TO THE SITE.
Report key: 8DFF10EA-8D55-471E-BEA0-CADAC7764377
Tracking number: 2ID-61126995

Attack on: ENEMY
Complex attack: FALSE
Reporting unit: Not Provided
Unit name: Not provided
Type of unit: None Selected
Originator group: UNKNOWN
Updated by group: UNKNOWN
MGRS: 38S MD08846867
CCIR:
Sigact:
DColor: RED

116th BDE reported that a UK convoy of 3 non-tactical vehicles and 7 pax was ambushed by 7-10 AIF with SAF and RPGs at MD 0898 7042. One British NTV (Toyota Land Cruiser) was disabled and no casualties reported. The British convoy moved south out of sector to FOB Danger and left the disabled NTF at the ambush site. BDE directed 1-163 to send a QRF to destroy the disabled vehicle and any classified documents/equipment remaining. 1-163 sent 2 platoons to the ambush site at 1322. 231302FEB05 116th BDE reported another Direct Fire Ambush. 145th SPT BN convoy was taking SAF at MD 082 688. They reported no casualties or damage. 116th BDE reported that two AIF vehicles moved west on ASR Orange from that grid. The QRF from 1-163 converged on the area and did not find any AIF activity. The NTV and sensitive items were recovered from the first ambush site. At 1415, BDE S2 reported that the white trucks may have been from a small village, MD 109 779. The QRF platoons were instructed to leave a security element at the ambush site and investigate the village. The elements moved to the village and two white vehicles fled as they approached. The QRF stopped the white vehicles and questioned the occupants. It was determined they were not AIF and they were released. The QRF RTB and brought the NTV to FOB Mc Henry. TF Griz will conduct counter-ambush operations on known convoys moving through the area, starting 24 Feb 05.

The American military said they couldn't determine the insurgent losses in our contact. However, there were blood trails from many locations, including the tower. There were also pre-prepared weapon and ammo points dug into the surrounding berms, implicating the Iraqi police, who should have been manning the checkpoint. The Americans also informed us that the insurgent cell's modus operandi was a hard and fast attack with the object of overrunning the team quickly. Apparently, an ex-Iraqi Special Forces major had about 50-60 Saddam Fedayeen paramilitaries in the area, and they were giving the Americans hell. Well-fed, well-trained and committed (as I had thought when I noticed the occupants of that black BMW), they were not typical Iraqis.

If we hadn't put up an immediate, coordinated return of fire, and had just initially carried out our usual cross-decking drills, where all of the occupants of one vehicle move quickly and orderly into a second rescue vehicle, they would have been among us with their vehicles and foot soldiers.

Although we were only seven men and seriously outnumbered, we had one belt-fed M249 Minimi squad automatic weapon (SAW) per vehicle, which was a much-needed force multiplier. They just weren't expecting such firepower, or for the small team to stand toe-to-toe with them. They knew the ground and our tactics, they knew the quick reaction force's response times and the clock was ticking. We delayed them and had probably been dicked (spotted) leaving the checkpoints earlier in Kirkuk.

We had been incredibly lucky to escape their pre-planned kill zone without injury. One American report stated 7-10 insurgents, which is laughable. I estimated more than 30, as they had two full pickups, four in the BMW and who knows how many already at the checkpoint. Everywhere I looked, there were enemy firing at us. Those American numbers were way out.

On our return to FOB Freedom, there was a bit of a fuss around our ops room. The boss and the head of the PCO team had set up a meeting of upper management to hand out letter of thanks to each of us for the two contacts that we had just been through. Although it meant nothing officially, it was nice to be recognised and something for my kids to look at in the future. My only gripe was that DK got one for the first contact, in which he contributed nothing and ran away.

ATTACK AT THE DEADLY "TREE LINE"

In March 2005, I moved from Mosul back to Baghdad. The company had lost its first man in a suicide car-bomb attack on Route Irish, the infamous road to Baghdad International Airport. I was to join that team and literally fill a dead man's shoes. All the Baghdad team's call-signs were Swordfish, and I was joining Swordfish 3, which shortly after became Swordfish 5, due to an unexplained name shuffle from the office. A guy called John Oliver was the team leader. All the lads were from different sections of the British military and gelled well. Our days were filled with long trips into the red zone, taking clients far and wide in the totally hopeless task of reconstruction. Occasionally, we did longer runs south and occasionally west to Fallujah and Ramadi.

On one of these Fallujah runs, we were hit hard at the notorious area known as the "tree line" on Route Mobile. A large building was being built on the south side of the road, and it was a known ambush point for insurgents. As we approached, heading towards Baghdad, everyone was alert and ready. I had two clients in the back of my Bravo vehicle. They were very quiet. Colin Walker was British, worked with the electrical reconstruction and was switched on to the situation, but the other was a US military female who had never been out on the roads of Iraq. She had missed her chopper to Baghdad and through the powers that be, had managed to bum a ride with us at the last minute.

The first indication of anything untoward was a large amount of dust splash on the right side of the road around the Alpha vehicle and the muted sound of small arms fire, followed by the calls of: "Contact right! Go! Go! Go!" over the radio. It's amazing how much sound is blocked out in an armoured vehicle, but the amount of incoming fire was increasing. Suddenly, we were the

141

target, as we passed. Bang! Bang! Bang! My vehicle was sledgehammered as we drove through the contact. Marcus Kennedy popped open the roof hatch on the Charlie gun truck behind us and began returning fire with the Minimi.

Once we broke contact and cleared the tree line, the team leader, who was Andy Ferreira, called us to stop and assess the damage, as all vehicles (especially the Alpha) had been hammered when we drove through the kill zone.

As we slowed to check the vehicles, a new round of small arms fire opened up from the right side of the road. "Go! Go! Go!" Charlie vehicle commander Neil W was calling us frantically on the radio to move. Unknown to our first two vehicles, the insurgents were now paralleling us and it had turned into a rolling contact!

We exchanged fire for a total of around 3km, and the Alpha vehicle was hit hard. Allan Kennedy was at the wheel and had been nursing it along while the rounds shredded his front brake system, rear side windows, windscreen, tyres, wheel arches, bonnet and so on. I drove through bits of his disintegrating Chevrolet Suburban for the full 3km.

Eventually, we broke contact and limped into the entrance of the infamous Abu Ghraib prison, pulling in to safety behind a blast wall, where we got out to check the vehicles over. They were in a shit state. The Charlie gun truck had a few holes but the most noticeable were three 7.62mm splash marks on the hatch cover that Marcus had been behind when he was returning fire with the Minimi. My Bravo vehicle had taken a round through one of the two fuel tanks. I was running on one Teflon run-flat disk because the left rear tyre was gone, and one of my two spares under the rear of the vehicle was totally shot out. All of our wheels were fitted with these disks – if the tyre burst, you just dropped onto the Teflon disk and at a reasonable pace, could continue for 50km or more. The damage that gave me the biggest headache was the round that had hit the rear door so that it was permanently locked! The two clients had to get out, and we manhandled the second spare wheel over the back seat and out of the rear passenger door.

Once the wheels were changed and the motors inspected, we set off for home via Baghdad Airport. We had a base there and they could offer assistance if necessary. I ran on the leaking fuel tank as long as I dared and with a little left to dribble out, I switched on to my good tank. Eventually, we made it back along Route Irish, through Checkpoint 12, into the green zone and straight into our daily ration of screaming C-RAM sirens, followed quickly by incoming mortars and rockets!!

When serving Americans were in a contact with us, they often would get us to sign written descriptions of the incident. This was to help them through the process of receiving a combat medal. It didn't matter that they were almost always basically baggage and contributed nothing to the day's outcome. The woman in the back of my vehicle that day was no exception.

One memory I have of having the vehicles repaired after a contact was watching six men struggling to lift a new armoured windscreen into my Land Cruiser. They were that heavy. I was told that they each cost $12,000 – and we got through a few. The armoured Land Cruisers weighed 4.5 tons.

The same route from Fallujah would provide some more fireworks on a separate mission. We were returning back to base after a recce behind the Abu Ghraib prison when the occupants of a saloon car parked 50 metres off the road opened their doors, jumped out and opened fire on our three-vehicle convoy. The rounds missed my Bravo vehicle and we followed Alpha under a flyover bridge that spanned the highway, Charlie vehicle was exposed to the gunfire longest, and our rear gunner on the day, Gary Pitchford, quickly cracked his vehicle's rear armoured door and returned fire. Once the Charlie vehicle was past the bridge and we had broken contact, we slowed and made it back into the green zone without further incident. The vehicles were all checked over and we saw how close Gary had been to stopping a round. About two inches from where his head had been were two 7.62mm holes from the insurgents' fire. The team had used up another life.

WE SHOT AN AMERICAN

Driving into Baghdad Airport, we shot a member of the American Special Forces. It happened like this. I had to drive a vehicle for another team that day because of lack of manpower. No problem, I thought. I got into my body armour, drew my weapons from the armoury then headed to the operations room for the pre-mission brief. Everything went as normal until I was told that one of our armourers, an American, was going to be rear gunner on the trip. He was to be dropped off at the airport as he was flying home.

All went well through Checkpoint 12 and along Route Irish, but the day took a turn for the worse as we approached a tailback of civilian traffic, stretching back from the highly fortified entrance to the airport.

Our military entrance was on the extreme right of the road and was channelled into what was in reality a narrow tunnel between two concrete blast walls. We drove straight into this lane and just as the Charlie vehicle was entering the blast walls, a black Opel turned sharply from its slot with the civilian vehicles and accelerated into our lane between the blast walls. An orange flag was waved to catch the driver's attention and flares were fired in accordance with the rules for use of force by the American armourer/rear gunner. However, the Opel continued to approach the rear of the Charlie vehicle. One warning shot was then fired into the road in front of the car and it came to a screeching halt. The driver jumped out holding his ID passes in the air and was yelling in a heavy American accent that we had shot his passenger in the foot. He was yelling that he was a member of the American Special Forces, walked to the rear of his vehicle, pronounced that he had an AT-4 anti-tank weapon in the back and was justified in using it against us! Most of the team members I was working with on the day were Columbian, and the calm, deep-voiced response from one of them, with his weapon levelled on the American was: "Try it."

144

The sign on the back of every gun truck

The American eventually calmed down and first aid was given to the wounded guy. The military police were called and before long, we were in the Special Forces camp. They were taking pictures of our vehicles inside and out. Suddenly, they rounded us up and told us to raise our hands. We went through the "Everything you say may be taken down in evidence and used against you," but that was about all they could do because they were completely in the wrong.

The investigation rolled on for a month or so. The American probably got his Purple Heart, leave back in the USA – and hopefully, they reviewed their Standard Operating Procedures for approaching the rear of a PMC convoy, where a huge sign across the doors told them to stay back 100 metres or risk being shot.

Rear gunner or "Trunk Monkey"

IED ON A BLACK ROUTE

One hazy Baghdad morning, we made our way up to the operations room for a briefing on a mission to Baqubah (Al Zarqarwi's hideout) 50km to the north-east. The job was to drive past a court building being constructed and grab as much video and as many photographs as possible. The Corps of Engineers overseeing the project wanted to see if the dollars were being put to good use. The team leader, Vandal Mclean, had put in the paperwork for the mission the night before. This was run past the US Military before being signed off and they updated us with any info that might affect us on our task – or that's what was supposed to happen.

The American military used a colour code for the various routes and roads around Iraq, with green being the safest colour and black the worst. What they forgot to tell us was that Route Pluto, which went past the bottom end of Sadr City, had been classed overnight as a black route. This meant that no military traffic was to travel on it. They knew something that we didn't, but forgot to tell us.

We set off out of Checkpoint One and crossed the Tigris River, heading for Route Pluto. I was rear gunner and as I was in the very back of the Charlie vehicle, I watched the oil ministry pass on my left side as I looked rearward. We turned left and swept down a feeder road onto Pluto, and I listened intently to Jason as he called out relevant info on what was developing in front of us.

Suddenly, he called out, "Roof tops 3 o'clock, John." I looked to see a group of dickers (watchers) on a fire station roof. As I watched, they faded back from the roof edge and Boom! We were hit with falling debris. The Alpha and Bravo vehicles disappeared in a cloud of dust and shrapnel. Alpha had been hit with an IED on their right side. Mac, the team leader in the front passenger seat, was temporarily deafened and the side of the armoured vehicle was a mess, but it was still drivable. We abandoned the mission, crossed onto the other side of the road, U-turned and headed home.

The damaged Alpha vehicle had been borrowed from another team because ours was being patched up from the previous Fallujah incident, so they weren't too happy when we finally limped into the car park.

Bravo ahead and Alpha enveloped by the IED blast – Sadr City

In another incident, we were taking military engineers to a water treatment plant in an attempt to supply the local people with clean drinking water. We were passing under a pedestrian overpass when I noticed a green plastic bag in the central reservation. Alpha vehicle passed it and as I was directly looking at it, it erupted in a large ball of flame and dust. Alpha took shrapnel in their rear and my windscreen was hit. I lost power steering and the air-conditioning died. We pushed on to the venue but my car was leaking various fluids, so we rustled up an armoured flatbed truck and it was carried home to the green zone.

WHEN
06/29/2005 0930
WHERE
AL MUTHA ALWAN – IN BAGHDAD
38SMB39459701
OUTLINE OF INCIDENT

IED – Explosion
Force: PSD
Target: PSD
DETAILS OF INCIDENT
An IED was located in a green bag and noticed at the last moment by a 3 vehicle PSD team as they were on their way to take a client to a project site in the Al Mulla Alwan area. The device was located on the roadside under a footbridge. The detonation caused damage to the first 2 vehicles of the 3 vehicle team but there were no injuries to the team or clients. 1 vehicle suffered a blown out tyre and the second vehicle had damage to the front radiator, windscreen and power steering.

When vehicles were badly damaged or written off in some outstations, we were tasked with driving new vehicles from our Baghdad base, sometimes to places as far away as Mosul, 400km north of Baghdad. We would run a gauntlet of IEDs and small arms fire along Route Tampa out of Baghdad, then take differing routes to get to our destination, hopefully arriving with no fresh bullet holes or worse.

Once delivered, we usually had to make our own way back. This usually involved bumming a ride on any Blackhawk heading in our direction. I loved these low, fast trips – so low that we had to hop over electric cables strung between the countless normally unpowered high-tension pylons covering the country.

Coming back to Baghdad from Balad

A MEDAL FOR MY MATE

We received a request one day to visit one of the many Baghdad ministries for discussions on reconstructing the electricity sector. We headed out of Assassin's Gate, exited Checkpoint One and crossed the Tigris. I was driving the Bravo vehicle, weaving through the heavily congested Baghdad traffic with constant radio chatter in my earpiece. We reached the ministry safely, a sliding metal door opened and all three vehicles drove in. The client was quickly escorted to his meeting and we then settled down with eyes on all of the entry points. Jason Appleton, my vehicle commander, said, "Quick, look at this bloke." Inside the compound, in the doorway of the building next to us, a young guy in his 20s looked to be in serious trouble.

Jason watching his arc

His arm looked severely messed up, so Jason said, "Watch my back," and got out of the vehicle with his weapon. He walked the few steps to the guy, turned around and headed to the rear of our vehicle, pulling out the med kit. The guy was obviously in a lot of pain. Jason cleaned his wounds, administered silver sulphide cream and wrapped the arm in plastic cling film.

It transpired that the guy had a tattoo on his arm. Because this was frowned upon in the Muslim world, he had decided to remove it himself with a soldering iron! He was too afraid to go to hospital, so this was the best treatment he was going to get. Jason gave him the rest of the tube of cream and cling film as the team leader's voice in our earpieces told us the client was on his way out from his meeting. We left Tattoo Man to his own devices and departed.

Back at base, there was a flurry of activity around our regional operations centre (ROC). We all mustered in a conference room where a podium had been set up. Our CEO began with an outline of how the company was doing and where we were going. He then invited a big American military officer on stage. The guy thanked us for the work we were conducting and said, "I would now like to do something that I have never done before. I will present a civilian with a medal. Would Mr Jason Appleton please step forward?"

Jason, who was standing next to me, walked up to the stage, blushing more and more with every step. The officer congratulated him, shook his hand and presented him with the Defence of Freedom Medal. Jason shook hands, received the applause and returned to my left side. While the officer was finishing his speech, he whispered out of the side of his mouth, "How much do you reckon I'll get on eBay for it?"

The medal had been given for an incident on the airport road, Route Irish, involving the first death within the company. A suicide bomber had swept down a feeder road, driven straight into Jason's Land Cruiser and detonated his device. Jason was blown out of his armoured vehicle and woke up lying in a puddle of water. His M4 was still inside the wrecked vehicle, which by now was a ball of fire, and he was receiving automatic fire from a nearby bridge spanning the route, but he quickly returned fire with his 9mm Glock, using the minimal cover of a palm tree that had been blown down in the blast. Eventually, the insurgents broke contact. Jason was shipped out to Germany to have his burned hands and arms treated. Twelve weeks later, he was back in Baghdad on the team.

ROCKET IMPACT

I was relaxing in my room, reading a book after a day in the red zone, when the C-RAM alarms went off, followed by the loud sound of a very close incoming rocket and an almighty crash. A 107mm Chinese rocket had been fired from the Haifa Street area and had hit the gable end of the building next to mine.

An American contractor had been lying on his bed about 40 metres from my room, reading like me, when the rocket hit the wall next to his bed, directly above where he was lying. Most of the shrapnel and brickwork was blasted over him and into the room, but he was still in a bad state. His door was internally locked and initially, no one could enter until James Williamson got a boost up from the outside stairs and clambered through the gaping hole in the wall to open the door from the

The Chinese 107mm rocket impact.

inside. He found the guy lying in the rubble and began immediate first aid by sticking paper towels into the hole in his head, before help arrived with a stretcher. The casualty was carried off to the neighbouring US military hospital and I never saw him again, though I heard he had speech and hearing problems after his recuperation.

THE BLACK MAMBA

I returned to Baghdad after a leave period to find a new member on my team. I will call him Dom. He was from Uganda. We soon found out that he had one really embarrassing trait: everything in his life revolved around the contents of his underpants. The guy was thick as a stack of planks and a complete liability. In every American base we visited, he would ask any passing female American soldiers, "Do you want some black? Check out my mamba!" It got to the point where a complaint was made and he was not allowed in any of the Morale, Welfare and Recreation (MWR) buildings that we visited while transporting clients around the country.

We were given a tip of the reason leading to his dismissal from his last security company. It seemed he had taken a picture of his "mamba", turned it into a Christmas card and given it personally with a wink to his female high-ranking American military client! This obviously went down like a lead balloon. Somehow, we ended up with him.

It got to the point where Dom's behaviour meant he had to go. On his next leave, he was asked not to return. As he was from my team, I was part of the group involved with clearing his kit from his room. This was where it became very strange. He had a massive supply of Viagra and had built a contraption that had only one purpose. It was a series of pulleys and weights that led to the ceiling on a frame and terminated in the groin area. It appeared to allow him to lie on his back and vertically stretch the "mamba"!

You never knew the minute that something would happen. Falling rounds (bullets) were a regular occurrence. One off-duty American soldier was making his way to one of Saddam's pools for an afternoon of relaxation when he was struck in the neck by a falling AK47 round, which had been fired indiscriminately from somewhere in Baghdad. Luckily, his friends were around and he survived, thanks to immediate first aid. Everything that goes up must come down, and even though a lot of kinetic energy has dissipated, the rounds still have enough force to kill you, as a local barber who had set up shop just outside of our compound found to his cost. He closed shop, walked out of his door and was struck square in the chest by a falling AK47 round. It had been fired in town from the Haifa Street direction, and found an unfortunate and innocent victim. Rockets and mortars were part of the daily menu. After a while, they become the norm. The only time they really caught our attention was if they landed close, because it meant there were probably a few more on the way.

THE CAR THAT HIT US HEAD-ON

In the later stages of my time in Iraq, my company were deploying South African armoured Reva vehicles. These were 8.5 ton beasts, but the only way in or out was through double doors on the back, or via roof-mounted twin turrets, in an emergency. They were built on Toyota running gear, and driving them any distance was a workout because of the intense heat generated and forced into the cabin.

One roasting hot summer day in 2007, I was wrestling my Reva around the narrow streets of the Karradah area of town, a South African team leader in my passenger seat. We had completed our mission for the day and were on the wrong side of the road, as the normal side of the road was congested, while the opposite side was totally clear.

Suddenly, in the distance, a car was driving straight down the centre of the road towards us. The team leader stepped up into the front turret and waved a Day-Glo orange banner to catch the driver's attention, then fired flares towards him. The Iraqi population knew to pull off the street if that happened: double-page spreads in Iraqi newspapers showed exactly the procedures to be taken around military or private security detail convoys. This was also regularly shown on local TV.

The guy never deviated or slowed; he just kept on collision course with my vehicle. The correct drill was to disable his vehicle with shots at the engine, followed by the driver if he continued. For reasons unknown, the team leader didn't complete the Rules for the Use of Force (RUF) by stopping the vehicle with well-aimed shots into the engine. I slowed but couldn't get out of his way. The car drove at a fast pace into my Reva and was effectively completely run over. We rolled to an alarming left angle but he was spat out of the back and had a second impact with the following Reva, which also drove over him. I often wonder if he was carrying a car bomb that never went off, as it was clearly a deliberate attempt to crash into my vehicle.

Amazingly, I saw him clambering out of the wreckage. We left it for the local police to deal with the aftermath.

It was known that there were people willing to climb into an empty vehicle (normally a taxi) and sacrifice themselves by driving fast into the back of a convoy. Iraqi TV crews would be pre-warned and film the whole event. The driver would be pulled from the bullet-riddled taxi and a quick sweep done with a camera to show there were no explosives.

My Battle Bus, the South African Reva

Then an outcry would go up. "Poor Ali! He was a good family man, trying to make ends meet." The local media would claim he had a tribe of children, was the perfect family man and so on.

It just wasn't true. He knew exactly what he was doing. We had transponders on every vehicle so we could always be placed at the scene of any incident during a review. Every incident was reported without fail by us, post-mission.

INSIDE SADDAM'S NUCLEAR BASE

I took part in a visit to the Tuwaitha Nuclear Research Centre, the main site in Iraq involved with handling nuclear material. It started life in 1967 when three main nuclear facilities and a waste location were put into operation. These were:

1. A French-built IRT 2000 research reactor

2. A radio-isotope production building

3. A dumping station. Many other nuclear facilities were subsequently constructed at this site.

We spent a very short time there. Instruments brought by clients showed a reading way too high for us to hang around. One of the two local Iraqi guys on my team had been stationed close by, in an anti-aircraft battery during the Gulf War, and confirmed there had been looting of the facility on an epic scale. He said this included nuclear material and isotopes, because it was believed they could be sold for a large amount of money. I wonder where they are now. They were never recovered.

Until 1991, the facility was a nuclear research facility and fell under the direction of Khidir Hamza. It was surrounded by a sand berm that was 50m high, and it contained the French-built but Iraqi-named Osirak research reactor, prior to it being destroyed by Israel in 1981. I was told that a Polish company had built the massive sand berm, a feat of engineering in itself.

It was fun to watch military clients and their escorts struggle to the top of the berm in helmets and full body armour in the Baghdad heat, while I looked on from my air-conditioned vehicle below. There was a lot of swearing and water consumed when they returned.

A party of US Marines discovered the Tuwaitha Centre in April 2003 and apparently told reporters, "We may have discovered a secret nuclear facility."

It was protected by American forces after the war and maintained by contractors from the Raytheon Corporation. Complete control was turned over to Iraqi authorities in the summer of 2004, just before I arrived in the country.

The locals never seemed to appreciate or really want any of the help being poured into their infrastructure. If pylons were erected to carry power lines, they would be blown up. New bridges would be destroyed, rebuilding of orphanages, hospitals, schools – and on occasion the kids or patients in them – would all be targeted.

The Iraqi people were given enormous amounts of aid. If they had allowed the West to help post-Saddam, they would be in a much better state than they are now. Tree-hugging lefties and couch commandos whose expertise is merely down to watching television irritate the hell out of me. I saw first-hand the terrible waste of resources due to an absolute hatred by the majority of Iraqis of anything Western.

KILLING THE ORPHANS

We visited one orphanage with two US "hearts and minds" female military personnel, and encountered the depths that insurgents would go to cause fear and chaos. On arrival, the clients dragged bags of teddy bears, bags of books, pens and other stuff from the vehicle. Within seconds, all hell was let loose. The kids went into banshee mode and the biggest kids (or young adults) won, carting off all the booty they could carry. Nobody from the West can grasp how chaotic it is in a third-world country when a crowd goes feral, until you are in the middle of it. The women we were escorting were in shock but insisted on going into the orphanage to talk to the leaders. Our standard operating procedure was a cut-off of 20 minutes at any venue. Anything over that, and we were asking for trouble on the way out.

Insurgents were very proficient at throwing a snap ambush together. These women were a nightmare. They were all teary-eyed around the kids and had to be almost manhandled back to my vehicle. We had been at the venue for 30 minutes and everyone was on edge.

I asked one of our local guys what the multitude of signs stuck on poles and walls around the orphanage meant. Apparently, they were advertising a kids' football match on the upcoming Friday.

We left the venue by a different route. The two women were dropped off unscathed (at least physically) and we parked and prepared the vehicles for the next day's missions.

The following Friday, I was crossing from my room to a friend's room when there was an almighty blast. I looked towards the source and saw a heavy black pall of smoke around Checkpoint One, which we had exited through the day before. I assumed it was a suicide bomber hitting the checkpoint again, but at the evening debrief, I heard the full story. The orphanage had held their football game as advertised. However, when the kids were all gathered in one of the goalmouths, scrambling to score or defend, an explosive device dug into the goalmouth was detonated. Both Sunni and Shia kids were killed and maimed. I don't know the numbers killed and injured, but I do know that we should have never have extended our time at the whim of those two women because we drew attention to the place for sure.

I remember very clearly an intelligence report that cemented the fact that insurgents had no limits to how far they would go to bring chaos. A girl with down syndrome was given a rucksack and told to take it into a pet market. Once she walked into the market and was surrounded by the hustle and bustle of people, the bomb hidden in her rucksack was remotely detonated. This was not the only time this method was used.

MEMORY OF A HUGE CAR BOMB

We were often moving and protecting a command sergeant major around sites in Baghdad, with some extended trips down south. He was the main man for the whole of the US Army Corps of Engineers in Iraq. A shout went out for us to head to our operations room, where we were briefed for a mission to Balad Airbase along the infamous Tampa North Route. We received the usual intelligence reports, weather and so on, then moved to the command sergeant major's compound. He was briefed on what to do in case of an attack, then climbed into my truck.

At first, the trip was uneventful. I was concentrating on the usual continuous chatter on my earpiece, when the distant blast walls of the airbase came into sight. A massive mushroom cloud of black smoke and flame rose into the sky from behind the walls. This was immediately followed by the shockwave and sound of a massive car bomb. Mac, team leader of the day, travelling in the Alpha vehicle, immediately ordered a U-turn on the four-lane highway, but insurgent fighters appeared out of the treeline opposite the airbase entrance and began firing into the area around the blast and towards us. A few leaped into a dark Opel car and pursued us, leaning out and firing from the car windows. This turned out to be a costly mistake, as our rear gunner immediately halted their progress.

Back in the sergeant major's compound, he got out of my truck and told everyone to wait while he collected something. On his return, he called everyone out of the vehicles and made a small speech about how we had saved his life on the day. He told us that he would like to give us a token of his appreciation, shook all our hands and deposited his own personal coin in each hand. These coins were only given when the owner thought that something exceptional had happened – they are not a medal but a personal token of thanks. Like the paper presented to me in Mosul, it was nice to get some appreciation for the work we did every day. That coin is still with my small bundle of items that remind me of those days.

The command sergeant major's coin

The end of 2007 was fast approaching. I had acquired a tongue-in-cheek reputation of being a bullet magnet by some, and had been in Iraq for over three years. I had been involved in 19 contacts of varying intensity and been rocketed or mortared day-in, day-out. I had been extremely lucky up to this point and sometimes, I wondered if the next bullet had my name on it.

To this end, I was casting my net to see what was next. Afghanistan was kicking off, and I seriously considered it, but what really caught my eye, because of my seafaring and security-related background, was an increasing incidence of vessels being hijacked off Somalia.

Chapter Five

BACK TO SEA – FISHING AND ANTI-PIRACY

HOW I NEARLY CAUGHT A SUBMARINE

I got home from Iraq on December 2, 2007. Even though I had my eye on the up-and-coming anti-piracy sector of security, I decided to fulfil one of my lifelong dreams. I organised a slick website, bought a fast aluminium Finnish boat and became a fishing guide.

The 23,000 islands outside of Stockholm were my workplace. It was great fun but hard work: very early starts and late finishing. I ran trips for Brits, Italians, Americans, Canadians, Japanese and every nationality in between. Most clients were lovely people, though a handful were hard to be civil to.

A Japanese guy was the funniest but most infuriating. I picked him up at his hotel in Stockholm and took him to the boat ramp from which I launched my purpose-built charter boat. I had tried to talk to him prior to picking him up, but his English was far from good. All I really understood was the hotel address. "I bring my own gear," he said, and "I like catch snakehead." I googled snakehead, a mean-looking Asian predatory fish, and decided he would probably like to try for pike as there weren't any snakeheads for about 6,000 miles.

After a boat ride to the hottest pike area I knew, I showed him a large rock protruding out of the water in the bay. I tried to explain that pike like to lie close to the rock and ambush small Baltic herring. I also explained that I had caught big fish consistently to the right side of the rock.

He pulled back his useless snakehead rod – and cast in the opposite direction! I tried to explain again and was met with a flurry of affirmative head nods, and "Yes, yes," followed by another cast in the wrong direction. As calmly as possible, I stopped him, took a more powerful rod and cast to the right of the rock. Bang! An immediate bite from a decent fish. I gave him the rod, and he landed his first pike, a fish of around 5kg. I took a few pictures and convinced him that killing the fish and taking it to the hotel to show his wife was a bad idea. Did he learn? No. He continued to do the opposite of what I recommended for the rest of the day!

I was trolling for salmon one day off Utö Island in the Stockholm archipelago. The sea was very calm, with a long north-south swell. I was far out, the shore just a thin line on the horizon. I was in the middle of making a cup of tea, with 11 rods pulling salmon lures at different depths, when I heard a very loud sound close by. I turned and a submarine had surfaced! It passed down my port side about 200 metres away and headed towards shore. I'm not sure they even noticed me.

My main concern was that I was towing two heavy lead balls connected to my 19-foot aluminium boat by thin but extremely strong wire cables. If either had caught on the sub, I would have been pulled backwards and probably under, if something didn't snap.

I was flicking through a UK angling magazine one day when I read about a British fishing journalist and documentary producer called Andy Nicholson. I knew he liked both pike and sea-trout fishing, so he agreed to come over to sample my area and write on my setup. He also brought a great character along called Keith Elliott. The two of them bounced stories off each other like Laurel and Hardy.

A nice salmon and my charter boat

They both managed to catch sea-trout and pike in the short time they were with me. A full magazine-style story of their trip was deposited in my email inbox, which helped me get a few more UK clients.

UNARMED BUT FIGHTING PIRATES

I survived my first year of fishing, but the news channels on TV were telling me that I should be elsewhere. I put a CV together showing my military service, 22 years of offshore diving and rigging work, plus nearly four of front-line security in Iraq, addressed it to a company in London, Armorgroup, that I knew was involved in the Somalian anti-piracy business, pressed the send key and waited.

Fifty minutes later, I got an email inviting me for interview. I flew to London and was told the interview was a formality: I had the job. Before I knew it, I was heading to Aden in southern Yemen to catch a ship heading east.

In the beginning, we were unarmed. I can hear collective groans of "And what use are you without weapons?" Quite a lot, actually. After checking my ship in with United Kingdom Maritime Trade Operations (UKMTO), which coordinated warships in the area, we organised a reinforced safe-room or "citadel", razor-wired the guard rails and carried out drills so the crew knew what to do in the event of an attack. I transited the Gulf of Aden in the early days of the Somalian piracy problem for Armorgroup on countless old tubs, but eventually ArmorGroup was bought out by G4S, so I moved on to freelance for various other security companies involved in maritime security.

At this early stage, the Somalian anti-piracy business was brisk. We were doing most of our vessel boardings through Aden or Djibouti. To get to the latter, I usually had to fly first to Addis Ababa or Nairobi to connect to the final destination of Djibouti city in Djibouti the country: Djibouti in Djibouti.

One of my most memorable flights was from Nairobi to Djibouti. As I walked up the boarding ramp to the open door behind the cockpit, I saw a beaming face looking at me from the pilot's seat with two thumbs up. I smiled and gave him the thumbs-up, though I secretly hoped that a cleaner had sat there for a minute to pretend he was a pilot. I loaded my bag in an overhead locker, buckled up and... "Ho, ho, ho... Good morning, ladies and gentlemen. This is Captain Karaoke. I am your pilot for today." The large head at the pilot's window matched the broadcaster's voice. My fears were confirmed. He continued his speech for some time with many ho, ho, hos thrown in, before his concentration was diverted from the microphone to the flight.

Once airborne, he never stopped talking. He was on permanent send until, thankfully, we started our approach into Djibouti.

I had landed here many times and always tried to sit on the right side of the aircraft. There was a scrapyard that we always flew over on the approach and an old grey MiG fighter was parked up in a corner of the yard. On this approach, the thing that caught my attention was the speed at which we were travelling. It seemed that we were flying a lot faster than we should have been just before landing. Suddenly, crash! We hit the runway, bounced, crashed down and bounced again. We came to a neck-wrenching halt, right at the extreme end of the runway.

"Ho, ho, ho! Ladies and gentlemen, Captain Karaoke again. I wish to apologise for the hard landing. However, the ground came up a little faster than normal today."

No it didn't. The ground never moved.

NIGHTMARE TRIP ON A TANKER

One of the anti-piracy companies that occasionally employed me was based in the UAE. I got a call to ask if I was available to act as team leader on one of its transits aboard a Chinese merchant tanker, the *Yuan Xiang,* which had recently been pirated and released in Somalian waters. I jumped on a flight to Salalah in Oman where the vessel was waiting and where I met the one other guy who would make up my "team".

The Chinese crew involved in the piracy incident were all changed out for fresh men and we set off towards Sri Lanka at an excruciatingly slow speed of 8 knots. The food was best described as diabolical. I had something placed on my plate that looked like a part of a predator's jaw – protruding teeth, the lot. I had no idea if it was animal, fish or bird. I went to the galley and with hand gestures, asked if I could cook something myself. I got the nod, so I found some eggs, beat them, dipped bread in the mix and fried them in a wok, It wasn't long before I had a queue of Chinese gents who also thought the cook's offerings were a disaster. The Chinese maritime chefs' course must be one of the hardest courses in the world, as after transiting the Indian Ocean on other Chinese vessels and sampling equally disgusting food, it was obvious that no-one had ever passed it.

The bread ran out two days later when coincidentally, it became extremely rough. A tropical cyclone was howling through and we had a cargo of iron ore. If allowed to become wet, such a cargo has sunk many ships because it moves and can roll a vessel over.

Our vessel was making strange creaking sounds every time we rolled. I wasn't exactly happy, as while off Somalia, another vessel had T-boned the *Yuan Xiang,* and it had a massive dent halfway down the starboard side.

At the end of one of my watches on the bridge, I was listening to an increasing loud creak from above the bridge so I went to investigate... and I couldn't believe what I was looking at. The

Somalians had stolen the bracing wires that steady the whole navigation mast, and as the ship was rolling to some scary angles, the welding on the mast's foot was splitting away from the parent metal of the bridge roof. I ran down and dragged the captain up for a look. He lit a cigarette, shrugged his shoulders and disappeared back into the bridge, He just didn't care, as the vessel was on a one-way trip to a Bangladesh scrapyard anyway. When my relief arrived on watch, I told him to stay in the centre of the bridge because I was sure the mast would collapse, He agreed and I headed down to my disgusting 40-degree centigrade cabin. The air conditioning, like most other things on board, was broken.

Four hours later, there was an almighty crash and the main engine stopped. There was chaos on the bridge. The massive steel mast had fallen onto the port bridge wing, and a cross member had gone straight through one of our only two serviceable lifeboats one deck below, rendering it inoperable.

The collapsed mast

After what seemed like an eternity of pitching and rolling on an increasingly angry sea, the engineers got the engine running again and we were instructed to head back to Oman for repairs. But that meant heading into the teeth of the storm with a mast hanging over the port side and our speed down to 6 knots.

We made it to Salalah and the company put us up in the Hilton while the vessel was being repaired. I've never been so happy to see a soft bed and a bath.

The one toilet on board was a precarious thunderbox that was hung over the side. It was one step from death at night when the ship was in total darkness. There was no toilet paper so I used an old notebook with its slippery A4 pages, I hate to think what the cook used.

The "thunderbox"

Eventually the old tub was fixed, reloaded with extra eggs and bread, and we set sail once more into the pirate-infested Indian Ocean.

The powers that be had finally woken up to my written reports, stating that because of the slow speed at which we were travelling, we could very well end up with the ship once again in pirate hands off Somalia. We hugged the Omani coast to a position off Muscat, where we dropped anchor and waited for divers to clean the barnacle-encrusted hull so the ship would slide through the water more easily.

We followed the coast of Pakistan then India, disembarking with great relief in a heavy swell off Galle in southern Sri Lanka.

I have travelled to many destinations around the Indian Ocean, and here's a tip for those who want to bring a halt to the illegal African ivory trade. Every Chinese vessel I worked on prior to leaving any east African port (excluding South Africa) always had a few visitors just prior to departure. They always brought ivory on board, which was sold to the crew. Sometimes there were very large quantities. I tried to alert port authorities a few times, but absolutely nothing happened.

It got to the point where it was obvious it would be better to keep quiet, as dockside authorities appeared to be fully aware of the sales and are as far as I could see, were entirely complicit in these illegal deals.

Aboard one of the tankers crossing the Indian Ocean

FLAT TYRE IN "INSURGENT CENTRAL"

One trip to Yemen involved a flight into the capital Sanaa, then a car ride through some extremely dodgy back streets with a former Royal Marine, Laurie Freeman. Once out of the ramshackle city, we pulled off the road and parked on the side of a hill with lights off, waiting in darkness for a group of Yemeni coastguard personnel to join us.

They turned up in a small Suzuki minibus and we headed for Hudaidah on the Red Sea coast. It wasn't long before we had our first problem. The minibus started to weave alarmingly and it was apparent that we had a flat tyre. We pulled over and the Yemeni coastguard was frantically trying to locate the spare, muttering some Arabic and in English: "Not good, not good, many bombs." I learned later that we had broken down in "insurgent central".

Later, when I told some French Special Forces guys who were familiar with the area, they couldn't believe that we'd got out without some form of contact. Eventually, a second vehicle pulled up behind us with wheel-changing equipment and various-sized tyres. The driver got to work, when from out of nowhere, a man stepped out of the darkness trying to sell us cigarettes, Coca Cola and the ever-present stimulant khat. This drug is a massive earner in Yemen for local farmers and is so popular that its cultivation consumes much of the country's agricultural resources. An estimated 40% of the country's very limited water supply goes towards irrigating it.

The tyre was fixed and a heated argument took place, as per normal, over how much the repair cost. A figure was finally agreed, money changed hands and we were on our way over barren rocky mountains.

As the sun came up, I was looking at houses perched on the side of the road made of piled-up rocks, and I wondered how these people survive. There was not a single shrub or blade of grass in the region – nothing. If any bombs are dropped in this region, nothing happens. It's just a stone-moving exercise. There is literally nothing to destroy.

We arrived in Hudaidah and were housed in a rundown hotel that had pictures of Prince Naseem Hamed, the former world featherweight champion boxer, all over the small foyer. From what I could make out, he had relatives in the area and had actually visited there.

Next morning, we boarded an ancient coastguard vessel that was to drop us off on our tanker, the MV *Agios Emilianos*, heading down the Red Sea from the Suez Canal. Our transport to the tanker must have spent its life alongside the jetty. Nothing was prepared for sea. Once they managed to start the extremely grumpy engines and left the harbour's shelter, everything was falling from shelves, tables and all storage areas. There was an almost constant sound of smashing crockery and glass as we rolled around.

The guy on the wheel was yelling in Arabic to a second guy on a radar set in the bowels of the ship to locate the tanker, but with no success. We were charging around in circles, checking various tankers in the anchorage, but they had no idea which one was ours. It got to the stage where I took over the VHF set, called the tanker and got its position and heading. When I passed this to the officer in charge, I might as well have given him the starting sequence for the space shuttle. He didn't have a clue. Eventually, they found a chart and I worked out where the tanker was, guiding the helmsman to our target. Finally we climbed aboard the tanker with our boxes of equipment and weapons.

The escort down the designated shipping corridor was uneventful, though we listened in to a long series of radio calls involving a French yacht off the Yemeni coast. A husband and wife thought it would be a great adventure to do a bit of east-to-west pirate dodging. He was shot dead and she was kidnapped.

Some people are so wrapped up in their bubble of "we are happy and harmless people, so everything is OK" that they don't realise what an evil world lurks out there. In my eyes, they are suicidal idiots.

I recall a German couple in late 2004 in Dahuk, Kurdistan who looked a bit "hippyish". They had two small children (girl and boy) and had decided to hitchhike the length of Iraq as a family adventure. This was at the height of the beheadings, where anyone from the West was a target. My team tried to talk them out of it and explained graphically what would happen when they were snatched. But they actually laughed at us. I always wondered what happened to them.

We disembarked the tanker off Nishtun, a border town next to Oman. In the harbour, we noticed a lot of skiffs, which could be harmless fishing boats or set for pirate activity. We suspected the latter. To compound this, we saw dodgy-looking alleged government officials, who were far from pleased to see two white faces.

Laurie, me and the Yemeni coastguard

They constantly went into a huddle and obviously discussed us while we were kept at a distance. Finally, we were told everything was in order and we hopped back into the minibus, which had been driven the width of Yemen to meet us.

We drove out of the harbour area in a cloud of dust, under an arch with an anti-aircraft gun stationed on each side, and set off on the coast road to Al Mukalla, which we knew to be a hot resupply town for pirates. We were heading straight into the lion's den, but at least we were armed. The coastguard had a couple of AKs strategically placed between me and Laurie, which gave some slight relief, but the minibus could hardly be classed as a fighting vehicle. After only 20 kilometres, we encountered the first hurdle: a roadblock. Yemen was like North Korea for travel: you needed papers to allow you to pass between a set of checkpoints, then fresh paperwork for the next set. We had been told to take a copy of our passports from the ship. However, these were taken from us at the first checkpoint, so we were constantly searching for cafes with fax machines, to satisfy the constant demand for various obscure documents from our office. Progress along this coastal route was excruciatingly slow.

During one toilet stop on the barren coastal road, one skinny coastguard was charging around like a madman in the tumbleweed scrub. He came back with a handful of big locusts or grasshoppers and held them out to me. I declined his offer. He shrugged, popped one live insect in his mouth and began chewing with obvious relish. The last I saw of the dust-covered insect was its long spindly legs disappearing down his throat. I asked the English-speaking commanding officer if this was normal. He looked at me as if I was stupid. "It's free food," was the curt reply.

During one of our five checkpoint legs, a black BMW drew alongside. The occupants took a long look, then overtook and screeched to a halt ahead of us. Our driver jumped out and taking some light cover from his door, had a heated argument with the BMW driver while resting his hand on his pistol. I had my hand on an AK and said to Laurie that if it kicked off, we had to debuss and head for a sand berm at the side of the road. As a former Royal Marine, Laurie needed no prompting.

Tense moments passed. The BMW occupants finally jumped back into their vehicle and sped off in a cloud of gravel and dust. I was convinced they were going to set something up ahead, but we made the next checkpoint without incident and after another paperwork shuffle, we could see the lights of Al Mukalla, where we were passed the night in a rundown hotel. We had to re-order our evening meal about four times there, as every time we tried to ask for a dish, the waiter would shuffle away and come back with the same statement. "It's off the menu tonight." Basically, they had no food.

The coastguard officer, who was very pro-British, told us about their training facility in Aden, funded by the British taxpayer and originally furnished with two old but functioning coastal protection vessels. A Royal Navy training team had been shipped to Aden with the vessels, and training commenced with the newly formed coastguard. After 12 weeks in the baking sun, it was time for the naval instructors to take some well-earned leave. However, this is where they made a serious error. They all went on leave at the same time.

On their return, they visited the training facility and more importantly, the two vessels. They walked up the gangway of the first and noticed something was not quite right. Both ships were riding too high in the water. They walked aft and were greeted with a gaping hole in the deck where the two gas turbine main engines should have been. The engines had been removed and presumably sold as soon as the training team had left Yemen. There were many raised hands and looks of feigned disbelief from the Yemenis, but no-one seemed to be able to work out where they had gone. As Aden was a major port, I would guess they had been trans-shipped and were heading east. The ships were used for dry training after that but fell into disrepair. They are probably both on the seabed by now.

The next morning, we slipped away into the small Al Mukalla airport, where an old burka-clad female took serious exception to the fading tattoos on my forearms. After trying to keep her calm for 45 minutes, our plane arrived and we flew back out to Sanaa where again we overnighted and made it home the following day.

Following Yemen, I had a period of flying around the world as a security consultant to various large shipping companies. I would conduct a review of their security lockdown drill (if they had one), amend it and inspect the ship, to advise how to set up a strong citadel or safe haven and implement anti-piracy measures. If required, I would also execute training in respect to running a full lockdown drill. Back home, I would write an in-depth review and submit it to the security company employing me.

BANGLADESHI MUD-MEN

On one trip, I flew to Chittagong in Bangladesh to inspect three ships at anchor and carry out crew training. I have travelled extensively but never seen the sheer volume of human beings in one place that Bangladesh holds.

I was driven to the Chittagong sea front, though I can't really call it a beach, because there was not one grain of sand to be seen. It was a glutinous mass of grey-black sludge that stank. The tide was out and the water's edge and my speedboat transport was approximately 100m from where I stood.

I asked the shipping agent how I was supposed to get to the speedboat. With a lot of head-wobbling, he explained that assistance was on the way. Two – for the want of a better description – "mud men" turned up. They were caked in the foul mess lining the sea front and each had what looked like a picnic bench with him.

After a lot of what appeared to be haggling, they set one bench in the mud and gestured for me to walk its length. I complied and the other bench was positioned in front of the first. They continued this until I had walked over the mud on the benches to the speedboat. Once my work was complete, the mud men were there for my return trip to the safety of land.

The taxi journey back was a real eye-opener. As it swerved through the teeming hordes of Chittagong, I saw a woman break away from the jam-packed sidewalk, step out into the street full of horn-blaring vehicles, motorbikes, rickshaws and donkeys, and squat down in full view of the population. She whipped up her dress and proceeded to lay down a big Richard the Third in the dirt. Once done, she just stood up. No wipe, nothing. Never missed a beat. Everyone just filed past. It was normal there. This summed Chittagong for me in one word: "Toilet".

BRAZILIAN BEAUTIES

I flew home from Bangladesh, then almost directly headed out again to Sao Paulo in Brazil. While waiting for my connecting flight, I went to a bar for a beer and got into a conversation with a young guy who spoke very good English with an American accent. While we were talking, young men and women kept coming up and asking for his autograph. Feeling a bit foolish, I asked who he was. Apparently, he was Brazil's best surfer, and was heading to the north to a competition. He asked where I was heading and more importantly, with which airline. I told him TAM Airlines and he laughed. His last words, as my flight was called, were, "The girls aboard are not employed for their brains." He left me wondering: so were they were all stupid?

As I walked to the plane entrance, I realised what he meant. Two drop-dead gorgeous Brazilian hostesses in what seemed to be spray-on white Lycra tops and blue skirts were welcoming me on board. I had to suppress pervert mode and not take a few pictures.

After an extremely enjoyable flight, a driver met me and we set off to Rio Grande. The Indian ship was loading up with grain and was absolutely covered in fat rats.

I was amazed by Brazil. Modern conveyor systems filled the ships and light aircraft were crop-spraying the enormous wheat fields. When we stopped at the immaculate highway's toll booths, the attendants were in smart uniforms. I noticed how many people, men and women, had blond hair and when I asked the driver, he said it was a leftover in that part of Brazil from Germans hiding there after the Second World War. He was adamant that Hitler had lived in South America.

I completed my survey/training package within 24 hours, said goodbye to the Indian captain and the driver whisked me back to Porto Alegre. Another enjoyable domestic flight to Sao Paulo, then the long flight home.

HAZARDS OF BOARDING AT SEA

A new anti-piracy company was asking for operators and I signed up with Gulf of Aden Group Transits, or GOAGT. It was steady work with a month on, month off, paid on leave rotation. We usually transited between Egypt and Sri Lanka or Oman to Sri Lanka and it was good fun. The company rented a staff house in Sri Lanka relatively close to Unawatuna Beach and the famous Banana and Hot Tuna bars, which went down well with the lads.

I went out with a few of the guys one night and after some beers, ended up in a late-night fast food joint. One of the ex-Irish Navy lads who the company employed was with us, chattering like a budgie. The Sri Lankan serving woman asked, "Would you like a pizza, sir?"

(Slurred heavy southern Irish accent) "Most certainly, madam, and as fast as you can fry it."

"What would you like on it?"

"Everything! I want everything on it!"

Fifteen minutes passed, with him slowly feeling more of the effects of last orders.

"Ok sir, it's ready. Shall I cut it into eight or 12 pieces?"

(Holding onto the food counter to stop the world spinning) "To be sure, oi'll never manage 12 pieces. Just cut it into eight!"

We were working in the Red Sea from Egypt to Yemen, around the Indian Ocean from Oman to Madagascar, Karachi to Durban and everywhere in between. It was fun but you had to keep your wits about you, as a regular trick while ashore was to spike your drink then rob you. I had a long conversation with a group of Kenyan police about this and they confirmed that people had even lost their lives to the scam.

Another hazard was embarking and disembarking ships at sea. The tanker, or whatever vessel we were working with, would steam slowly ahead and hopefully offer us a lee on the vessel we were boarding from. But if the vessel we were boarding was empty of cargo, it would be sitting on the ocean like a big cork and would roll heavily in a swell. As we went alongside, it would often crash against the superstructure of the smaller vessel, so if you were climbing a ladder to the tanker's deck, you could be crushed like an insect. Over the years there were several deaths involved in this operation. One guy fell from the ladder to be crushed between the ships. The swells at the southern end of Sri Lanka were often huge so it all depended on perfect timing.

I was employed as team leader on the company's many transits, but after a couple of years, I started to get a bad feeling about the way the company was being managed. So I finally left anti-piracy work in Durban, South Africa. Good thing I did. A few months later, the company went bust due to massive mismanagement. Operators were left with no salaries and worse, no way of getting home unless they bought their own tickets.

Chapter Six

NIGERIA

....

THE SLEEPING POLICEMAN

It was 2012. A friend from my Iraq days working in Nigeria was leaving his position, so he gave me the nod and I sent off my CV for his desk-bound security job in Port Harcourt. I was to fill the position of offshore security advisor for the Nigerian arm of Agip, the Italian Oil Company or NAOC. I was accepted and caught a flight to Africa.

The job entailed writing security plans and procedures, and running the general logistics for a number of offshore security vessels manned by the Nigerian Navy. The job was good, with two other expat guys in the office and constant banter. One incident soon after I arrived showed me quickly how the

Nigerian mind has a special way of covering for mistakes and not just coming clean. We had a policeman guard on the main door into our building. He seemed to think that sleeping the days away was an essential part of his job description. One expat photographed him sleeping. The expat thought this was maybe not enough, so videoed him too. He took this footage to the policeman's boss and explained the problem.

The policeman was called in and asked what it was all about. He picked his teeth with a toothpick and didn't seem to have a care in the world. The expat explained that he was sick of the guy not doing his job and produced the time and date-stamped photograph of this policeman reclining at his desk with his eyes closed. "Sir, I knew you were there, but I blinked when you took the shot!" The expat showed him the video clip and asked how he explained that. "Sir, I knew you were there when you videoed me. However, I was praying."

Next day he was back at the desk and fast asleep again. He's probably there to this day.

After a couple of years, the oil company decided that offshore piracy levels didn't warrant the cost of a security advisor, so I found myself back home again just before Christmas, jobless and with an uncertain future. But the offshore piracy continued.

INTO THE SWAMPS

After six months off, I was offered the post of security/risk advisor back in Nigeria with the same company but based in Brass Oil Terminal in Bayelsa State and the swamp area of the Niger delta. I was to manage all aspects of security for five flow stations, an offshore tanker-loading point and Brass Oil Terminal itself.

In a normal situation, all locations would be serviced by road. However, as everything under my supervision was in an enormous swamp, all logistical movements were carried out in the labyrinth of mangrove-lined waterways by tug or barge, supported by military gunboats. This was a brain-melting, stressful task in the beginning. Any problems seemed to involve pushing the default button, which was "security".

A cleaner had not been paid on time? Contact security. An old boat had taken on water in the harbour and sunk? Contact security. It took a long time to break that pattern.

There was more paperwork than I had endured in the past. I say "endured" because paperwork has never been one of my favourite tasks. (And here I am, writing a book!) I am more "hands-on", happiest dealing with situations and fixing problems instead of being stuck in an office.

SNAKES AND JUJU

The oil terminal spread over a large area with untouched forest in the centre, named by the local population as the Seven Sisters. Locals feared this forest and I never went in there myself. Its inhabitants included large numbers of snakes and they were all dangerous. The clinic had anti-venom shots, though some of the snakes were of the constrictor variety and very big.

I didn't mind non-venomous big snakes, so I got involved in catching the pythons that would attempt to pass our anti-climb perimeter fence. They were often were far too large to get through and would lie in the grass at the foot of the fence. If you are confident, it is easy to catch them. They are predictable and tire easily. Basically, you get them to strike at a forked stick a few times, then place the stick firmly behind their head and replace it with a good firm grip. Admittedly I only got involved with pythons up to around 2m. Everything over that size was left to the resident snake catcher.

My driver, Dickson Douglas, burst into my office one morning, shouting, "Sir, sir, a python has caught a dog." Four dogs from the nearby community used to squeeze under a perimeter fence gate and spend their day scrounging food. One had walked along the edge of the Seven Sisters and a big python had nailed it. We could hear the bush thrashing and the dog's cries get weaker until it was obviously dead. This was a dog around the size of a border collie. This variety of python can grow to 100kg, so it is not something to mess with.

When incidents happened around the terminal or outlying flow stations and a report had to be written, some of the local names used to amuse me. I recall especially Willie Dateme, Festus Longhorn, Cashmoney and Mens Magazine. We also had many Fridays, Sundays and Mondays but I never met a Wednesday or Thursday, for some reason.

Although predominantly Christian in the south, juju and strange cult beliefs still have a serious grip in Nigeria. One of the country's main newspapers gave a report of a cat that was arrested in a house, because a burglar had been seen entering a house but not exiting. When police arrived, all they could find was the cat, so they arrested it and locked it in a cell, waiting for it to transform back into its human state. This also happened to a goat that strayed into a courthouse. Security arrested it because someone had put an ID badge around its neck. They thought a human had changed into a goat.

Even well-educated people told me that if a man had the correct juju spell, bullets fired at him would stop in his clothing and he could just shake them out. I tried to explain the reality behind this but it always fell on deaf ears. Another popular one is that hunchbacked people have mercury in their hump. Albinos have a massive dollar sign over their heads – their body parts are worth a lot of money to do with all manner of juju. Cannibalism is also still around, as is the sale of body parts. As I write, I have just been sent a video of three men arrested for butchering and dissecting humans for juju rituals.

The Nigerians have an interesting Nigerian way to see if a child is eligible to go to school. (They have to be at least six years old.) You make the child put an arm over the top of their head and touch the opposite side earlobe. If they can accomplish this, then they are at least six years old and are eligible to enrol in class.

We carried out regular lockdown drills in case of any militant or terrorist attack. One local chief, who professed to a love of whisky, was visiting me on one of the never-ending attempts by locals to figure out ways of getting petrol from us. Looking at me through bloodshot eyes, he told me a story about how his father had been the voodoo chief of the area. After his father had ritually scarred his body and stood down, his son had taken over the reins. He whipped off his shirt and turned his back to me, revealing impressive intricate symmetrical scarring all over his back.

He then announced that he was going to give me a voodoo gift. It was a shell with a spell on it. If the terminal was ever attacked, I was to hold the shell to my lips and say, "Hide me." I would then be invisible to my enemies. I told him that I would use it at home to make a large withdrawal from a bank, but he informed me that it would only work against people attacking me when my life was in imminent danger.

He added that I must be very careful with it, as if I said, "Hide me finish," I could never come back and would never be seen again. "I will bring it to you tomorrow, boss," were his departing words as he left my office.

Sadly, I never received or even got to see the magical shell over the next few years, despite my many reminders to him.

SERGEANT SANDY (RIP)

The military or joint task force (JTF) that I worked closely with were housed on a large floating houseboat in the terminal's harbour with hot and cold-running prostitutes. The terminal doctor told me to have a word with my guys, as whenever a soldier went to the sick bay, they would be tested for HIV. The failure rate was very worrying. I got as many together as possible and gave them my best speech. This resulted in a complete ignorance of what I was telling them. They were like school kids sniggering, so I left them to the very likely prospect of a slow death. I found it extremely odd that even though the HIV statistics were through the roof, no-one talked about it. Many times I heard of someone getting "sick" and passing away, but never once did I hear of anyone dying of AIDS.

After my unsuccessful lecture trying to explain the dangers they all faced, I glanced over to a small generator barge that powered the houseboat, and saw a small brown-and-white dog hiding behind a coil of rope. I sat down on a weight-lifting bench and didn't look at him. Slowly he crept towards me and I felt his nose touch my fingers.

I asked what his name was. The soldiers looked at me as if I had gone mad. "Sir, he is just a dog, named Dog." I explained that I had a golden Labrador at home called Monty who lived in my house and that I bought food for him. They couldn't grasp the concept that someone would pay to feed a dog. "They should find their own food" was their attitude.

Finally, they said his name was Sergeant Sandy. I was soon his best friend. Whenever I drove to the jetty, he would jump up and down. He looked like a little fox and in one week, I had taught him to sit. The next trick was to teach him to give me his paw. But it was time to take my six weeks' leave.

On my return, I drove to the dock but there was no happy dog to greet me. I asked where Sergeant Sandy was. The soldiers looked everywhere except directly at me. It transpired that the

dog was there for one purpose only. When I headed home, it was hit over the head with an iron bar and turned into pepper soup.

Every day was filled with problems. Or, as Nigerians say, "wahalla." One constant recurring problem was the food, or "chop". No chop, no job. It seemed no military person in Nigeria was capable of missing a meal and continuing to work in an emergency. Everything had to stop so they could eat.

I have no idea how the Army fight Boko Haram in the north when it comes to lunchtime. Maybe that's why Nigerian Army sustain heavy losses. "Hang on, Mr Haram; we'll be back to fight at 14.00, because it's 12.00 and chop has just arrived."

The Nigerian military were used in various roles around the delta. All movements to any flow station (where the oil is pumped out of the ground) in my area had to be by water. The JTF, a ragtag mix of Army and Navy, used heavily armed gunboats to achieve this. All movements to the oil-producing flow stations had to be escorted by a minimum of two gunboats. They normally carried .50 calibre machine guns on the bow and an automatic 40mm grenade launcher at the stern. They would on occasion hit illegal oil refineries, take out any resistance where possible and burn the place back to water level. As the bunkerers had turned the place into a quagmire of mud and oil, this fire was the best way to get everything back to a semblance of normality. After about 18 months, their scorched-earth tactic didn't take long to turn the area back to its emerald-green natural state again. The jungle is truly amazing at repairing itself.

Wiping out the illegal oil refineries

Whenever telemetry was showing a large loss of oil, or an explosion or fire was reported along the vast pipeline system, we instituted an overfly. I would grab my chopper comms set and camera, and head to the helipad. Sometimes, we would catch the criminals or militants red-handed, trying to escape the chopper in a canoe. On many occasions, I wished for a door-mounted machine-gun but had to make do with my camera and GPS. This was definitely a case where the pen was not mightier than the sword, as the same problems kept recurring. Illegal oil bunkering is a massive drain on the oil companies' efforts. Bunkerers try to pierce the thick oil pipe on the very top in the 12 o'clock position, because the pipe contents are a mix of oil and water, and the oil floats on the water. One method was a hand-held grinder to make the pipe thin and flat, then a series of spot welds around a 2-3in valve. Spot-welding doesn't create much heat. (Remember, this was a live pipe and many died doing this.) Once a valve was completely welded to the pipe and fully open, they would smash a steel spike into the thin pre-flattened pipe until it was pierced. As soon as a good jet of oil was flowing, they would close the valve and connect a hose, then fill containers or in some cases empty boats with the crude oil. This was transported to one of the many illegal refineries hidden in the thick bush, and converted into rough diesel and petrol – or "cooked".

A captured illegal refinery showing a complete disregard for the surrounding environment

Nigeria as the biggest oil producer in Africa and is among the largest in the world. Yet it has to import most of its petrol, diesel and petrochemical products. A 2018 report revealed that despite huge resources expended on maintenance, none of Nigeria's four refineries worked at up to 50 per cent of their capacity at any time during 2017.

I have heard a lot of people talk about how the West should act towards countries living in poverty, especially in Africa. I have never been part of this "politically correct" nonsense that has swept the planet. But look at the facts. In a continent of over 1.2 billion people, Africa is unable to produce an airplane of its own; it doesn't make or export a saleable African car or truck, not even a TV or mobile phone. Yes, they may bring in phone parts and assemble them under a different name but they don't physically engineer the essential components.

196

I suppose a few cars, to be fair. But all of them are a joke, built from other countries' parts (mainly cheap Chinese). If you look hard, you'll find the following:

- The Kantanka (made in Ghana)
- The Innoson (made in Nigeria)
- The Kiira EV Smack (made in Uganda)
- The Mobius II (made in Kenya)
- The Turtle (made in Ghana)

Not exactly well known, are they? Google them and you will see why.

The "do-gooders'" battle cry is almost always, "Education is the answer. We need to bring education to Africa to help them grow their crops." But here are the facts. About 30% of Nigeria's population of 195.8 million people work in agriculture. As an example, a village chief with 100 working men is given the opportunity to send his best man to Europe to be educated in operating of the latest hi-tech tractor. Once he has mastered it, a tractor is donated by a well-meaning charity. The man and the tractor are then shipped back to the village. As it's the traditional time to prepare the ground prior to planting the crops, the chief orders the man to go out with the shiny new tractor and plough the fields. Everyone in the village is excited until they realise that one man is working and 99 are now only watching and earning nothing. Once the land is ploughed, the driver returns to the village and after a couple of weeks, fits what is essentially a large rake to the back of the tractor. He then drives back out to the fields, levels the field and 99 men stay home with no money.

Next comes planting, followed by the harvest. The tractor does it all. The chief is very happy because he is only paying for one man and some diesel. But he now has a major problem. Those 99 men are very angry at being out of work. They have resorted to drinking and squabbling because they have no way to support their families. The chief is now in danger of an uprising.

Suddenly, the tractor has a problem too. A warning light has come on. The trained driver has been told what to do in this situation. He pours in more oil. However, viscosity and brand names mean nothing in Africa. If it is slippery, it's good enough, so even though his Western education told the driver/operator otherwise, a mix of different oils goes into the hi-tech diesel engine.

The driver continues to work but it is not long before other warning lights and alarms come on. Eventually, the tractor grinds to a terminal halt. The chief can't find anyone who understands the computer systems on his shiny new tractor, so he rips out the fancy hydraulic-sprung seat and uses it as his throne. The batteries go to his house to power his radio, and the tyres are burned to fuel his oven. The tractor is taken apart piece by piece. Pipes, radiators, alternator and so on are used elsewhere, then its skeleton is abandoned to the bush, to rust and decay.

Those 99 men go back to work, earn a salary and the village is once again, in the Nigerians' words, "cool and calm".

That, my friends, is the true Africa.

My view: just leave the local people alone and stop pressing Western values at an impossible speed on people who are mostly tribal subsistence farmers and who have been living the same way since time began. The land can only support a certain number of people and because of Western interference, the population is already overtaking what the land can provide.

I have read and spoken of these views to a number of Nigerians in the country. They all nod their heads and agree that this is exactly how Africa is.

An army of grass cutters worked within the oil terminals and flow stations in the Niger delta and beyond. They were bent over at the waist all day, every day, and cut enormous areas of grass with machetes. My first thought when I saw them was, "Get them a lawn mower." It was explained to me that a lawn mower would put people out of work, so it would never be tolerated. In fact, it would be intentionally and terminally broken on the first day of use. Any modern-day automation over basic labour just will not work when a vast amount of the population are living on under $2 a day.

If anyone wants to make a huge difference in Africa, try to halt the rampant spread of HIV by teaching local people the importance of using a condom. Another key improvement would be to stop people throwing garbage straight out of their homes. Snakes, rats and vermin love it and breed profusely. Still, these rodents can be used as bush meat for "chop".

Then, and only then, get them to follow your teachings. Once that education has been completed and is being followed, then come back and talk again about further education.

Chapter Seven

GOLD

A LIAR AND A CHEAT

During time off from Nigeria, I began looking for gold in a few places in Sweden. I had tried it with Catrin back in 1995 in Småland and we both really enjoyed it. I can't remember what made me try it again, but once I found a couple of specks of the yellow stuff, the fever was back, and this time with a vengeance. I bought a pan, then a hand suction pump and sluice. Next came a motorised pump and high-banker, followed by an American dredge. I worked my way through all of the different methods of separating gold from Mother Earth, including rock crushers.

After a while, I realised the gold equipment sales market was like the fishing market: designed to catch a potential prospector. I sold all of my slick gadgets and concentrated on the well-proven basic tools. This led to a 2016 trip above the Arctic Circle in Finland and the goldfields around Ivalo and Kuttura.

A few guys I had met in the Swedish gold-prospecting world were in Finland and had put together a claim called Skäggwood, which literally translated from Swedish means "Beardwood". I had a great two weeks living in the Finnish wilderness, cooking on an open fire and fishing for native brown trout and grayling while prospecting. After driving the 1500km home and dreaming of going back, I was asked by one of the claim owners if I wanted to purchase a part-share in the claim. This was fun but it all fell apart when Alex Holstad, whom I had paid for my part of the gold claim, was uncovered as a scammer and con artist who stole from close friends.

One of the shareholders. Pelle, had spent the whole summer on the claim and ran equipment up and down a zip-line stretched between trees down a deep ravine to a stream. When he left, he did not dismantle the zip-line. The Finnish mining authority paid the claim its annual visit to check that everything was in order. We got word back from Alex that the zip-line had been left up and we had been fined €6000. Everyone was understandably furious with Pelle. However, after a check with the mining authority, when we realised that Alex was a serial con-man, it turned out they had only asked us to dig the dry toilet a little deeper for the following season. There was no fine.

It was obvious where the money had gone. When cornered, Alex could produce no evidence of the mining authority asking for €6000 – just a faked Photoshop bank transfer to the mining authority.

Long before he was uncovered as a con artist, Alex had put an idea to me to go 50/50 on our own commercial gold claim. I agreed and we secured a claim close to a gold-producing area called Tankavaara. I fuelled the van, drove up with a friend and prospected the area. I then paid half of the permits and applications for the claim to Alex, as he was fixing the paperwork. I also paid for half of an excavator. It all fell apart in 2018, when I realised he was scamming a lot of his friends. I had been repeatedly asking for email correspondence with reference to buying the claim for two years and alarm bells were shrieking. After visiting the Finnish mining authority's offices, I discovered that he'd never submitted any claim and that there was no excavator. The mining authority were very helpful and confirmed that he had been doctoring emails supposedly sent to them, in reference to a claim he had applied for a couple of years earlier. I was 75,000 Swedish kronor (more than £6000) out of pocket. I am normally a good judge of character but Alex Holstad was up there with the best thieves: very, very convincing.

The final straw was two water pumps that I was buying for the claim. Alex had sourced them in his village, so I paid him for them and he told me he had paid the owner (whom he worked for occasionally). I was told to come down with a trailer and pick them up any time. This was when his web of lies was falling apart. I contacted the pumps' owner, who said that he had not been paid at all. Alex had taken my money, and organised for me to, in essence, steal them. The owner would never locate them in northern Finland, and Alex would spend the cash.

What I should have done was an in-depth Google check on him. Seems like he had done it all before when he was in a heavy-metal band. The only amusing part of all this was that during an online session to find out more about him, some very interesting – how shall I put it: "gentlemen's entertainment" – videos popped up of his wife. She, incidentally, is a teacher who openly professes to hate children and (complete with a pentagram chest tattoo) openly talks of worshipping Satan.

As I write, I heard that his wife was spreading the news that he had jumped in front of a train. But a check on suicide reports on the railway system flagged up nothing in Sweden at that time. There was never any indication of a funeral either. He has just gone to ground for now. But I haven't forgotten.

FINDING A CLAIM

This did not put me off gold prospecting. Once Alex had been outed as a con-man and a police report lodged, I switched to putting my own commercial gold project together. I started looking at possible land and excavators to work it. I had built a one-ton 26in trommel – a mechanical screening machine used to separate materials – during 2017 and transported it to Finland in preparation.

At this point, I had a stroke of much-needed luck. A claim owner gave me the opportunity to work his claim in exchange for a percentage of the gold found. The two guys who would work it with me tested the ground and the results were very impressive, after a combined sluice-run of 25 hours. It was full speed ahead to secure an 18-ton machine permit for the 2019 season and sign a contract with the claim owner. The claim was available for me to work the following season. I headed back to Finland on another 3,000km round trip, finalised it all and everything was set.

During this trip with a friend, I prospected a remote piece of ground that I had studied for a long time. We stuck our pans in the creek and the first three I washed had lots of garnets and a very impressive amount of gold in them. Finally, something was going right.

Nuggets from the test holes

After working out the projected amount of gold per ton, I hastily applied to claim the ground but was told that someone had got there a day before me and submitted paperwork to claim it. I think that they were possibly tipped off that we had been there, prospecting. Up there, the forest has eyes. I then hired the services of a local geologist, who helped map out a claim a little upstream. At this point, someone told me it was "claim poker", so I named the claim "Kaikki Peliin", which is Finnish for "all in".

Once the ground was claimed, I began to search for a suitable machine to dig gold from the ground. An ideal setup was two excavators: one small unit to feed the trommel and one large one to feed the material. I also needed a hopper truck to transport the material between the two excavators. One conveyor belt to give a steady feed rate into the trommel and another to lift the tailings into a big rock pile would finish off a perfect set-up. But at this point, my pockets were not as deep as they had been, due to Alex's criminal enterprise. I settled on a Swiss Army knife of the construction world, a 1970 Norwegian Hamjern 766 backhoe.

This machine was being restored but the old guy doing the work had died. As far as I knew, there was no working clutch, no steering servo pump and a front hydraulic ram was leaking oil.

One of the two guys who was going to work on the claim for me got a price for transport up to Örnsköldsvik, an hour north of the backhoe's location, so I paid to have it transported there and it went into storage over the winter.

The clutch problem was not as serious as I had feared. Basically, the linkages had not been coupled together, but when coolant was added, it ran out of a hole in the bottom of the radiator as fast as it went in. An old Volvo radiator was hooked up and took care of that issue.

The leaking tilt ram for the front bucket was removed and we ordered two new matching cylinders. We planned on

My homemade 1-ton gold trommel

converting the trommel to chain-drive from two Kevlar belts. A CAD program was used to draw up the sprockets, which were cut and hardened. All was going well with the checklist:

✓ Van to live in
✓ Trailer
✓ Signed contract to work the claim
✓ Three water pumps and associated hoses

- ✓ Backhoe
- ✓ Two generators
- ✓ Trommel
- ✓ Custom 400mm x 4m sluice
- ✓ Rock slide for the trommel exit
- ✓ Tools
- ✓ Tarpaulins
- ✓ Containers and buckets
- ✓ Fuel containers
- ✓ Chainsaw

The main gold digging weapon, Goldie

The biggest thing left to do before the start of the season was transporting the backhoe that final 900km to the goldfields. An advertisement in a Swedish Facebook transport group hit bingo. We tied up a deal to take the backhoe, or "Goldie", to the gold fields. I was all set. What could go wrong?

FALLING FOUL OF THE POLICE

My van was totally loaded by the end of May 2019. The trailer was hooked up with my two big diesel pumps on board and I waved my family goodbye. I headed north on my adventure to the Finnish goldfields. About 90 minutes into my journey, I noticed a police van in the central reservation. I thought nothing of it until I noticed in my mirror that he was drawing alongside me. He gestured me to pull into a checkpoint that had been set up ahead. I pulled up behind a Dutch truck and confidently waited for him to check my details.

He worked his way to my open window and said: "Can I see your licence, please?"

"No problem, officer. First time I have ever been stopped," I replied with a smile.

He checked my licence and looked ominously at me. "Sorry, but you have a problem, my friend."

Apparently, I was driving a van registered as 4200kg, when my licence only allowed me to drive a vehicle up to 3500kg. I had absolutely no idea, and I could see that he believed me.

But I was now unable to drive. He climbed in, told me that I was never to drive the vehicle again without the correct licence and, in a gesture that I genuinely thank him for, he drove it past the inspection area and into the parking area at the exit just before the highway. It turned out that anyone with the same licence as mine but who had passed their driving test before 1996 could drive the van. I had no option other than to call my wife to drive it home.

After a couple of calls, one of the guys who was going to be working with me turned up in his car. We transferred the trailer to his car and he headed up to Finland. Catrin drove my van back to Stockholm. I then borrowed a "legal" Mercedes Sprinter from my brother-in-law and loaded all my equipment into his.

There was scarcely a centimetre of spare space when we had finished.

Bust!!

I left a few hours later for the second time and tried to make up time. As I approached Haparanda in the north of Sweden, I got a warning on my GPS app that I was approaching a speed camera. Up to this point, the speed limit had been 80kph so I slowed and checked the speedometer. Flash! I had just passed a 70kph camera at 76kph. That resulted in a speeding ticket for 1500 kronor (£125). Things weren't going well.

I caught my friend and my trailer up 1300km later, close to our final destination. On arrival, we caught up with some much-needed sleep.

The backhoe had been dropped off the transport truck at a nearby car park, so I was keen to get it to the claim. A quick inspection, however, showed a river of hydraulic oil running from the main back-lifting boom, so we abandoned it and headed to the claim to prepare the area for digging.

The third member of the team arrived a few days later and the backhoe was started, hydraulic oil added, then it was driven to the claim with its leaky digging arm. The only solution was to remove the main lifting hydraulic cylinder piston, order new seals and wait. It turned out that the seals could not be sourced in Scandinavia, so an order was made to Germany, which involved an even longer wait.

We began preparing the rest of the equipment, built a temporary workshop/storage area and bought drums of diesel from a Russian who was meant to have been on the Kursk submarine when it sank in 2000, killing all 118 on board. His wife had been sick so he was given leave to look after her – an illness that saved his life.

The trommel was pulled into position and the chain drive welded on. This caused no end of problems, which were eventually partly cured by just lifting the trommel a few more centimetres at the feed-end. For some unknown reason, the trommel barrel wanted to walk uphill, even though all the roller wheels were straight, causing the drive chain to jump off.

Finally we received the new seals, refitted the hydraulic cylinder and ran some paydirt for an hour. The result was just under 3.5 grams of gold, with some nice little nuggets. This equated to around $1400 for nine hours' work, though we faced the age-old gold miners' problem of trying to keep everything turning reliably for nine hours.

Unfortunately, I had to return home to go back to my job in Nigeria. This meant another 1500km drive before I headed to Africa. When I reached home, I was greeted with the news that the backhoe had almost died on us – the right-side back wheel was not driving and was wobbling very badly. It sounded like a half-shaft problem and the bearings were almost certainly toast.

A couple of days before I left for Africa, I was given an option to swap my old Finnish fishing boat for a nice Swedish 34' boat called a Riwall. I quickly drove my boat the six hours up to central Stockholm and the Australian owner of the other boat drove to my berth.

I was trying to sell my boat to fund an excavator for the gold-mining enterprise, so the swap was a good deal. That Swedish boat was like a small floating apartment and would be lot easier to sell than my old boat.

UNFORESEEN PROBLEMS

I waited nervously for reports on the claim's progress. Our Finnish claim neighbour also needed mechanical work done on his excavator, so one of my guys did it, in return for borrowing the machine when the neighbour was not around. This was a fantastic deal because our backhoe needed some serious work to make it mobile again. The two guys worked like hell to produce a mountain of paydirt and from the pictures I was receiving, the ground looked amazing: textbook gold ground with Ice Age sediment showing. It was frustrating to be so far from the claim. I wanted to be back badly, but my security job was the cash cow that fed the operation. My parents, who were being sent all of the info and pictures of the claim, were a great help when finances became tight. My mother wrote, "Better you get it now than when we pop our clogs."

At this point, the bills started to arrive for my own separate Keikki Peliin claim. These had to be paid almost immediately. I paid the first two but the final payment was a deposit into a bank account, giving the Finnish mining authority full access to the money. This account was a holding fee in case I did not put the land back to the required standard once mining was completed. It can then use the money to put it right.

But for my part, I could only access and remove money from the account with the mining authority's permission. Try explaining that to your local bank!

I tried, oh I tried. I showed the bank emails from the Finnish mining authority but after much scratching of heads, they refused to do it. I called a few Finnish numbers and found out that I could open an account in a Finnish bank and deposit the money there. Armed with this information, I approached the recommended Finnish bank and was immediately refused.

Nothing is easy when it comes to gold mining.

Finally, I found a bank close to the gold claim in Ivalo that was willing to open an account for me. The necessary amount was lodged and hey presto! I was the owner of my own gold claim. I had basically paid for the right to recover all of the mineral deposits on a 5.2 hectare patch of planet Earth. All I needed to do now was find gold.

The claim

A couple of weeks after I arrived in Nigeria, I got word that the two guys on the claim had irreparably fallen out. My Finnish gold-mining dream had once again come to a grinding standstill. Not only that, but the mechanically minded one of the pair had walked away and the tractor's back wheel, which had a broken wheel bearing, had still not been fixed. Oh, and the trommel needed some welding love.

The one thing I had inadvertently omitted from my planning was the human factor. Since I was 16, I have always worked in small, tight-knit teams, where conflicts got resolved. I had forgotten that many "ordinary" people just don't seem able to work together, laugh problems off or sort out any disagreement.

Nothing could really progress until I returned to the claim.

I was back from Africa in August 2019 and heading north to the conclusion of a mining season that never really got started. My plan for spring 2020 was to buy a more up-to-date excavator to avoid breakdowns and to use the tractor as a stationary feeder for the trommel. Once back at the claim, however, things took an unexpected but advantageous turn. Three people apparently owned it, and as I was trying to sort a contract for the next three years with one of them, another was negotiating with other miners to move onto the ground immediately. Luckily, I had not signed anything, so I pulled the plug and within six hours of discovering this, I was offered a new claim with no such complications.

So that is where I stand now. I have bought a working shaker wash plant, I have the use of a 3.5 ton feeder excavator and I have just bought a 21-ton excavator as the workhorse. The dream is still slowly moving forwards. I <u>will</u> succeed because my mindset is: never give in.

I might write a book of my gold-mining endeavours in the future, but until then, it's just hard work. Onwards and upwards.

A LAST WORD

So there it is: a few stories from an extremely condensed 58 years. I have no plans to stop working until I physically can't continue, so when that happens, I will think about a second edition of this book. Because of my present line of work, there are many things that I cannot put down on paper. When I finally leave the security industry, I will have time to reflect and add a few more stories and experiences on topics that I can't talk about now.

In my teens, I thought I would be involved in a war, that I would break a bone or two and be in prison at some point. I have no idea why, but I always knew. I thought I'd missed my chance of a war when I left the Navy and the Falklands kicked off in early 1982, but it's funny how things play out...

I was also convinced that I would become proficient with a musical instrument, so I have just bought a banjolele! Strange choice, I know, but they have always secretly interested me and George Formby can't be wrong.

This was my first attempt at writing a book, so I had to take time over researching the finer points. I often thought that it would be easier to write fiction. While penning a book of memories that span decades, it's difficult to get everything right. If there are any discrepancies, I apologise. But everything is written as my memory and limited research serve me.

Everyone has a book in them. When a person dies, a library of memories and stories dies with them. So go on: write a few headings, then fill them in. Before you know it, you will have the framework. You may even enjoy it as much as I have.

I've enjoyed writing this so much that I am well into my first crime thriller. Watch this space.

Over the years, I have enjoyed so many laughs and colourful characters in both the diving and security worlds. Many of the guys who crossed my path have passed away. The danger and after-effects can easily catch up. Their boots are, however, filled by equally crazy people, and I have generally found both jobs a joy to be involved in. The main problems (as in all work situations) seem to come from higher up the ladder. But enough said on that topic for now.

I have often had people ask, "Weren't you scared?" But hand on heart, I cannot recall ever being frightened after I completed my clearance diving course (apart, perhaps, from Kenny Kenyon's driving). My kids used to think that it was annoying because they could never scare me or make me jump. If anything happens suddenly, I immediately switch to analyse-and-act mode, which I think comes from my diving days.

When something happens at depth, you are the only one who can sort the immediate problem out. You cannot shrink back and allow others to move in. You are dangling on a thin umbilical which is a collection of your breathing gas, hot water and communications under a multimillion-dollar ship and are completely at the sharp end. I am no way trying to portray myself as any kind of superman or hero but this is just the truth.

On the minus side, I don't seem to be particularly good at emotion and sympathy. I can sympathise with the badly injured, but only after the initial treatment stage and when they are stable. Prior to that, emotion has absolutely no place in the proceedings. If it's toothache, a cut or some other trivial nonsense, I have no time for it. You will survive: just push through it. In my book, that gets much more respect than whining.

I have been around campfires and tables with people who seem to think it would be a good idea to talk politics after a beer. To my mind, this topic should be shunned in a group that's having fun unless they want the evening, or even a friendship, to be destroyed. My experience is that it never ends well.

My biggest annoyance is someone telling me something that I know is a lie, in an attempt to make their life or deeds appear more interesting. I just cannot agree and let it go. I prefer to stop it there and then, and "out" them in front of everyone. I don't really care if people are offended or embarrassed. Just don't try to bullshit me.

So cheers to all of you who have crossed my path over the years. I have no real regret over any of my choices. They have all combined to get me to where I am today. Here's to the next few decades. Hopefully, when I grow up, I too will live to a ripe old age like my parents.

If you would like to see to see a few videos of my time in Iraq and other places, check out the media section of http://www.johnsteeleauthor.com

GLOSSARY

AK47 – Russian-designed 7.62mm calibre assault weapon.

AT-4 – An anti-tank weapon made in Sweden and used extensively by American ground troops.

Banjolele – A cross between a banjo and a ukulele made famous by George Formby.

CDBA – Clearance divers breathing apparatus. A rebreather diving set that can be used without tell-tale surface bubbles.

Conkers – A game played by two players, each with a conker (horse chestnut) threaded onto a piece of string: they take turns striking each other's conker until one breaks.

Collet – A ring that tightens on a burning rod to hold it in the burning torch.

C-RAM – An alarm system that can detect incoming mortar rounds and other projectiles.

Crossdeck – Evacuation of personnel from a disabled vehicle to operational vehicle.

Debuss – To alight from a motor vehicle.

DSV – Diving support vessel.

EOD – Explosives ordnance disposal or bomb disposal. An explosives engineering profession using the process by which hazardous explosive devices are rendered safe.

Exfil – In military tactics, extraction is the process of removing personnel when it is considered imperative that they be immediately relocated out of a hostile environment and taken to a secure area.

FOB – Forward operating base.

GPS – Global positioning system.

HESCO – A large container made of a collapsible wire mesh outer and heavy-duty fabric liner inner. These are normally filled with sand.

IED – Improvised explosive device.

JTF – Joint task force.

LRRP – A long-range reconnaissance patrol, (pronounced "lurp"). A small, well-armed reconnaissance team that patrols deep in enemy-held territory.

MT – Motor tug.

MV – Motor vessel.

MWR – Morale, Welfare and Recreation. Buildings in all American bases for use by the troops for recreation, cinemas etc.

Overfly – A pipeline check from the air (helicopter).

Peshmerga – Meaning "those who face death". The military forces of the autonomous region of Kurdistan region of Iraq.

PKM – Belt-fed Russian light machine gun.

QRF – Quick reaction force.

Riffles – An obstruction in a sluice that allows low pressure to drag gold into its vortex and keep it there.

ROC – Regional operation centre, where all mission planning takes place.

RPG – Rocket propelled grenade. A 40mm Russian-designed rocket launcher.

SAW – Squad automatic weapon. We used the 5.56 Minimi.

SBM – Single buoy mooring. Tankers tie to these enormous buoys to fill or offload.

Scran – Navy term for food.

SD20 – Seaman Diver 20 – my course number.

SLR – Self-loading rifle.

Sluice – A steel or aluminium channel with riffles built in to catch gold.

Swarfega – A detergent used for removing oil from skin.

Trommel – A large rotating drum that washes rocks and allows the small particles drop through a series of holes onto a sluice below.

UAE – United Arab Emirates.

Wadi – A valley, ravine, or channel that is dry except in the rainy season.

A Wet – Naval term for a drink, tea, coffee or alcohol

Wren – The Women's Royal Naval Service (WRNS; popularly and officially known as the Wrens).

IRAQI MAPS

TURKEY
SYRIA
IRAN
SAUDI ARABIA
KUWAIT
DAHŪK
ARBĪL
NĪNAWÁ
AT TA'MĪM
ŞALĀH AD DĪN
DIYĀLÁ
AL ANBĀR
BAGHDĀD
WĀSIŢ
MAYSĀN
KARBALĀ'
BĀBIL
AL QĀDISĪYAH
DHĪ QĀR
AN NAJAF
AL MUTHANNÁ
AL BAŞRAH
Diyarbakır
Batman
Kurtalan
Hakkari
Mardin
Cizre
Zakho
Dahūk
Viranşehir
Al Qāmishlī
Al Ḩasakah
Sinjār
Tall 'Afar
Mosul
Arbīl
Ar Raqqah
Dayr az Zawr
Kirkūk
As Sulaymānīyah
Bayjī
Tikrīt
Sāmarrā'
Ḩadīthah
Al Qā'im
'Akāshāt
Hīt
Ar Ramādī
Al Fallūjah
Al Ḩabbānīyah
Baghdad
Ba'qūbah
Mandalī
Ar Ruţbah
Karbalā'
Al Ḩillah
Al Hindīyah
Al Kūt
Al Ḩayy
Al 'Amārah
An Najaf
Ad Dīwānīyah
An Nukhayb
As Samāwah
An Nāşirīyah
Al Başrah
Az Zubayr
Umm Qaşr
Al Fāw
As Salmān
Al Buşayyah
'Ar'ar
Rafḩā
Hafar al Bāţin
Al Jahrā'
Kuwait
Ra's al Khafjī
Tabrīz
Orūmīyeh
Marāgheh
Mahābād
Saqqez
Zanjān
Sanandaj
Kermānshāh
Īlām
Khorramābād
Borūjerd
Dezfūl
Khorramshahr
Ābādān
Iraq
International boundary
Governorate (muḩāfaz̧ah) boundary
National capital
Governorate (muḩāfaz̧ah) capital
Railroad
Expressway
Road
0 50 100 Kilometers
0 50 100 Miles
Lambert Conformal Conic Projection, SP 29°30'N / 36°45'N

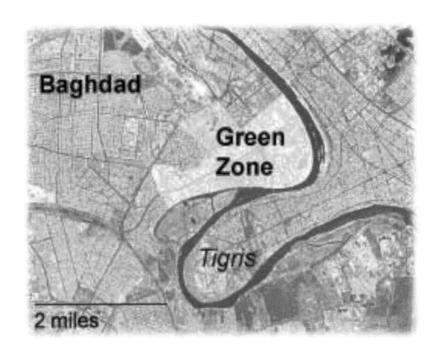

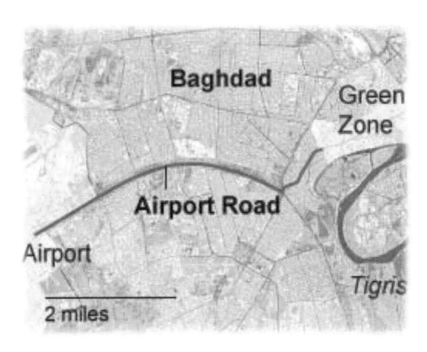

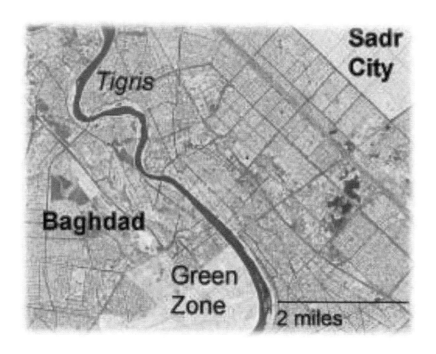